The World's Finest

An Elegant Tribute to the World Class Companies
that bring us the Finest of Life's Luxuries

MICHAEL H. CALDWELL
Creative Classics Inc.

The World's Finest

ISBN: 0 9692129 8 4

Credits

Book design and layout – Donna Szelest
Chateau Lafite photography – Keiichi Tahara
Crystal Cruises photography – Crystal Cruises
Pebble Beach photography – Joann Dost
Sonora Resort photography – Randy Lincks
Stone Brewing photography – John Schulz
Treetops photography – Craig Robertson & Rob Tucker
Trump Hotel photography – Michael Kleinberg
West Coast Fishing Club photography – George Fischer

Printed in Hong Kong by Elegance Printing and Book Binding Company
www.elegancebooks.com

Published by Creative Classics Inc., British Columbia, Canada
www.worldsfinestbook.com

Table of Contents

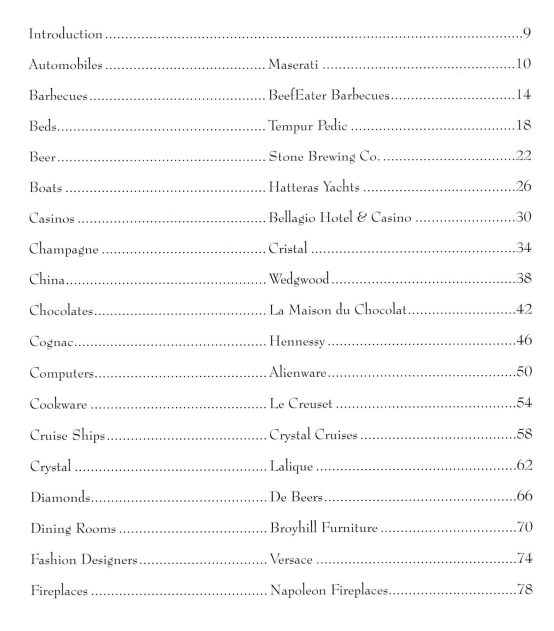

Introduction

This book was borne from the simple desire to create something beautiful and timeless for those people who celebrate 'the good life.'

The search for the companies showcased in the book involved countless hours traveling through the electronic ether and an almost equal number talking on the telephone. Information gathered from numerous upscale publications and online consumer opinion polls all helped in this effort.

The selection process for many of the products profiled was actually quite easy. When you think of certain luxury goods, there are landmark names that automatically come to mind – Tiffany for jewelry, Wedgwood for china, Cristal for champagne, Lalique for crystal, Versace for fashion design, Rolex for watches and Chateau Lafite Rothschild for fine wine.

Other choices required more research. Some might wonder at the choice of Maserati for automobiles, instead of sports cars. That was decided after discovering that the prestigious Robb Report's recent "Best of the Best" competition for luxury sedans awarded first place to Maserati's Quattroporte Sport GT.

As you browse through this publication, one thing will become clear. All of the companies featured offer unparalleled quality that is unequivocally synonymous with the life of luxury. Each of them is known as the best in class in today's marketplace.

In summary form, the chapters explore these companies' beginnings and their journeys onto the world stage. Corporate histories span more than three centuries – from Chateau Lafite (1680) and The Homestead (1766) to Alienware (1996). Company locations span the globe… from Scotland to New Zealand and from the United States to Japan. Their luxury offerings include everything from a $100 bottle of champagne to a $100 million yacht.

Maserati

Introduction

Maseratis don't sit still very often, but when they do they usually end up surrounded by appreciative—if envious—onlookers. Few automobiles in the world denote luxury, quality, and the fast life like a Maserati.

The Company

Like many youngsters in the early 20th Century, the six Maserati brothers of Bologna, Italy were thrilled by automobiles. Ultimately, five went into engineering, while the sixth became an artist. In 1926, three of the brothers developed and built a two seater race car with an 8 cylinder engine—the first Maserati automobile. Above its radiator was a badge designed by Mario, the artist brother, bearing the trident that remains Maserati's symbol today.

The Maserati brothers began producing race cars, and, from the beginning, the cars were all about speed. One of the first Maserati autos won the 1926 Targa Florio, a major race. In 1929 a new 3.5 liter world speed record was set by a Maserati V4 with a V16 engine. In 1933 Maserati won three European Grand Prix victories.

In 1937 the brothers sold the company to the Orsi family, who soon relocated Maserati headquarters to their hometown of Modena, where it remains to this day (albeit in a new factory). Over the ensuing decades the company changed hands a few times. Today it is under the control of Fiat, Italy's largest auto manufacturer, which also owns Maserati's rival, Ferrari.

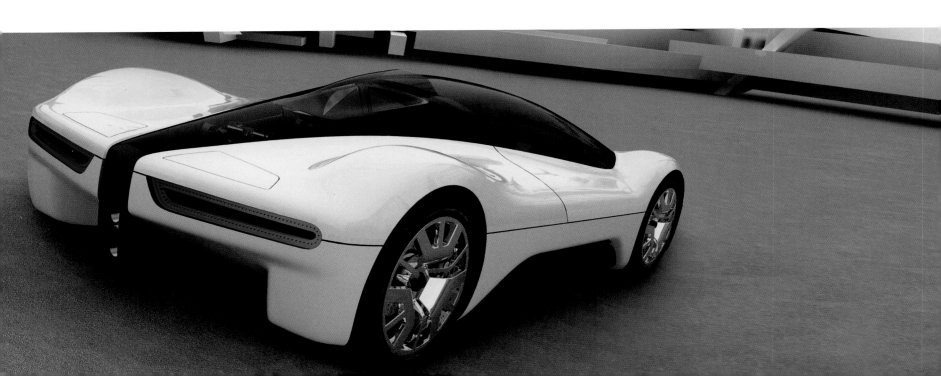

The Quattroporte's interior is the perfect extension of its exterior styling. The cabin is crafted from the finest woods and leathers. The exceptionally long wheelbase offers occupants plenty of room to stretch their legs, electronically adjustable front seats with 14 different settings are standard, and the driver's seat comes with three memory settings. In the rear, electric seats are independently

The Products

The new Maserati Quattroporte is the first Maserati designed by world famous automobile stylist, Pininfarina, in 50 years. A luxury sedan for those who love sports cars, the Quattroporte is the ultimate embodiment of beauty, elegance, sophisticated engineering, sporty temperament, and alluring exclusivity.

The Quattroporte's styling is unmistakably Italian: elegant yet aggressive, devoid of fussiness, with fluid lines and a body as agile and well muscled as an athlete's.

adjustable for reach and tilt. So many other thoughtful features have been added to the interior of the Quattroporte that it offers all of the comfort of a genuine limousine.

But most limousines don't offer the kind of Maserati luxury found in the Quattroporte, such as the refrigerated compartment nestling in the front armrest, the electric sun shade for the rear window, and an endless list of lavish features.

For all its luxurious limo comfort, the Quattroporte—especially the Sport GT Quattroporte—is a vigorous sports car, accelerating from 0 to 100 mph in barely 5.2 seconds and quickly powering to a top speed of 165 mph. That's thanks to a normally aspirated 4244 cc 90° V8 engine.

Given the world class features found throughout this phenomenal automobile, it was nice to see the Maserati Quattroporte Sport GT recently receive the highest of honors. It won the prestigious *Robb Report's* "Best of the Best" competition for luxury sedans.

BeefEater Barbecues

Introduction

The BeefEater story began in 1984 when founder Peter Woodland established Woodland Home Products with just $10,000 in start up funds. Just over 20 years later, BeefEater Barbecues has become an Australian and international success story, in which one man's vision for a better product has evolved into global distribution of the world's finest outdoor barbecue systems.

Modern design, quality materials and award winning innovation have earned BeefEater Barbecues pride of place on the patios, back decks and outdoor entertaining areas of barbecue chefs the world over.

The Company

An uncompromising approach to materials quality and construction techniques rapidly made them a hit with the local Australian market, and the BeefEater brand and reputation for quality was established.

Similarities between American and Australian lifestyles whetted Peter's appetite for challenge, and using extensive borrowings and expanded production capacity he set his sights on the US market. At international trade shows in the late 1990s Peter secured his first contracts for exporting barbecues to the United States and Europe.

And in 1991 the BeefEater Signature series barbecue was awarded the prestigious Australian Design Award for ergonomic design and the innovative glass viewing window.

The Products

BeefEater barbecues are stylish, high quality outdoor cooking appliances. Built to last with functional design, solid construction and durable finish, a BeefEater barbecue gives free reign to a chef's culinary skills and creativity.

Today Woodland Home Products is an international business with a turnover of more than $30 million; almost half of this in sales of BeefEater Barbecues to American and European distributors. In 2001, BeefEater was the outright winner of the Western Sydney Exporter of the Year Award, and runner up the two previous years.

During the Sydney 2000 Olympic Games, BeefEater was selected by the New South Wales Government to be part of the Australian Technology Showcase as an example of innovation and technology.

With its dazzling, all stainless steel construction, the top of the range BeefEater Signature SL4000s barbecue features four or five burners, an integrated side burner, a stainless steel roasting hood with viewing glass and warming rack, Quartz Start ignition on each burner, stainless steel plates and grills, the innovative Vaporizer® AntiFlare grids to reduce flare up, and high capacity stainless steel burners (18,000 BTU).

Standard inclusions for the stainless steel trolley are three storage drawers, condiment rack, ice bucket, gas cylinder enclosure, paper towel holder, side shelves, external storage racks and towel rail.

The BeefEater Outdoor Kitchen takes the BeefEater Signature barbecue series to a new level to create the ultimate in outdoor entertaining. With one or more Signature series barbecues providing the heat, the Outdoor Kitchen features modular cupboards, drawer systems, choice of bench tops, and provision for fridges and sinks, side burners, and cylinder enclosures.

Tempur Pedic

Introduction

Tempur Pedic International manufactures and distributes Swedish Mattresses and Neck Pillows made from its proprietary, pressure relieving material, Tempur. Conforming to the body, this material provides support, helps alleviate pressure points, and self adjusts to the body's shape, weight, and temperature. Tempur Pedic's products are currently sold in 60 countries, making it the world's leading manufacturer, marketer, and distributor of viscoelastic and premium mattresses and pillows.

The Company

Headquartered in Lexington, Kentucky, Tempur Pedic's high tech story begins with NASA's attempt to develop a material to relieve astronauts from the tremendous g forces inherent in lift off. Recognizing the vast potential of such a material as a sleep surface, the company spent nearly a decade of experimentation and millions of research dollars in developing the pressure relieving material known today as Tempur.

They achieved their goal. In 1998, NASA recognized Tempur Pedic for successfully using NASA technology to create economic opportunity and promote a better quality of life for humankind in both the consumer and medical sector. In addition, the company has been licensed by the U. S. Space Foundation to use the official "Certified Technology" seal on its product packaging. Only products that result directly from space technology and research are permitted to use this seal.

Bringing the high tech revolution into the most intimate part of the home—the bedroom—Tempur Pedic has improved the quality of life for millions.

Two luxury mattresses lead Tempur Pedic's lineup, allowing customers to choose a bed and sleep style geared to their own needs and tastes. As if to underline their quality and value, both beds carry a 20 year limited warranty.

Extravagant design and unsurpassed luxury define the GrandBed, which takes bedtime comfort and luxury to new heights. Beneath the plush, blended silk cover are four layers designed to pamper a body. First, a comfort layer

The Products

Tempur Pedic's mattresses are a high tech alternative to the 80 year old innerspring mattress design. This breakthrough in sleep technology self adjusts to each person's body, distributing pressure over the entire surface of the mattress. Tempur proves that a mattress can be both firm and soft—firm where you need it and soft where you want it. These revolutionary mattresses offer unprecedented luxury and comfort, virtually eliminating painful pressure points and reducing a body's need to toss and turn in search of a comfortable, pain free sleeping position.

of high density material assures the ultimate in support and pressure relief. Second, another layer provides edge to edge therapeutic support. Third up is a layer designed to increase air circulation. Fourth, a base layer provides support from below with a high resiliency foam base. The GrandBed offers unmatched pressure relieving comfort and body conforming support.

The superbly comfortable Classic Bed offers support and comfort layers made

from Tempur material that rests on a long base layer designed to increases air circulation. The Classic Bed has won the esteemed Ease of Use commendation from the Arthritis Foundation.

Travelers hooked on Tempur Pedic can cruise the world in comfort with the Travel Set—a terry velour covered portable mattress overlay and Travel Neck Pillow, both slipped into a convenient weatherproof duffel bag.

Stone Brewing Company

Introduction

Craft beer is made from a traditional process that blends sugars from malted grains (wheat or barley, for example) with hop flowers and water. The end result depends on the skill and taste of the brewmaster, who nurses the fermentation process along to obtain a desired aroma, color, mouthfeel, foam, and flavor quality. Most craft beer is not pasteurized. Often (though not always) it goes through a filtration process. Yeast may remain in the bottle as a sediment.

The end result is a beer that—like a fine wine—offers a deep, complex flavor. Hop flowers can contribute the scent of citrus, flowers, or herbs, while barley may offer up the aromas of caramel, sweet biscuits, cocoa, coffee, honey, and even cookies. Beyond this, certain yeasts can contribute flavor characteristics such as clove, spice, banana, strawberry, or apple.

Of America's craft beer makers today, none receives higher or more consistent praise than California's Stone Brewing Company.

The Company

Stone Brewing was founded in 1996 by two college students. Steve Wagner, a musician, and Greg Koch, who ran a music rehearsal studio, had known each other briefly in 1989, but then lost touch. A few years later, at UC Davis, they found themselves together again in a class entitled "Sensory Evaluation of Beer." Renewing the friendship, they began to pursue their common interest: beer.

Eventually they hit upon the inevitable: why not start their own brewery? After pulling together enough seed money, they founded Stone Brewing. Things weren't easy at the start, but after a couple of years the company stopped cornering the market on red ink and began showing a profit.

And then suddenly Stone Brewing was being hailed as one of the world's top craft brewers, averaging annual increases that ranged from 30% to 40%. In 2005 the company moved from its original building in San Marcos to new facilities in nearby Escondido.

The Products

Approach Stone's brews as you would an excellent wine. Hold your glass to the light, observing the depth and nuances of color. Take in the aroma, trying to sort out the complexity. Finally, take a small sip, allowing the beer to rest in your mouth while you analyze the bouquet. What flavors alight on the palate? What kind of mouthfeel do you experience? What sort of finish does it offer?

Stone offers a variety of craft beers to suit most tastes, but it is particularly

renowned for its full bodied, sometimes bitter brews.

A good example is the award winning Arrogant Bastard Ale, with its pronounced levels of bitterness and alcohol, and its hints of fruit and floral aromas. At 7.2% alcohol, this ale packs a punch in more ways than one!

One of Stone's special brews, released only once each year, is the Imperial Stout—consistently ranked by experts as one of the world's greatest beers. Dark—nearly black—it's delicious, heavy on the palate, and offers generous hints of anise, black currants, chocolate, coffee, alcohol, an overall roastiness, a creamy mouthfeel, and a smooth finish. According to Greg Koch, Imperial Stout, if stored properly, will age like wine, growing increasingly more complex.

Stone Brewing is also noted for its three classic ales. The flagship Stone Pale Ale is deep amber in color, robust, and alive with the flavor of malt and hops. The India Pale Ale, originally developed in the late 1700s by Britain's breweries for shipments to troops in India, is intensely hopped and nicely bitter. And the Stone Smoked Porter—dark, rich, complex—offers a nice amount of peat smoked specialty malt.

Hatteras Yachts

Introduction

Back in 1959 at Cape Hatteras, North Carolina—where nor'easters can blow almost as fiercely as hurricanes, thanks to the collision of the frigid Labrador Current and the tropical Gulf Stream—Willis Slane dreamed of building a boat. It would be no ordinary boat, of course, no wooden fishing boat. It would be rugged and robust, capable of conquering the area's unruly waters and wild weather. It would be all of that, yet at the same time it would be the greatest sportfishing boat available. In a major break with the wooden tradition, Slane chose to use a new material called fiberglass to build his dream boat.

The Company

Hatteras Yachts produced its first sportfisher, the Knit Wits, in 1960 (the Knit Wits is still in service today). A 41 foot twin cabin sportfisherman with a 14 foot beam and a pair of 275 hp Lincoln V 8s, she received an enthusiastic reception and the company was on its way.

Two years later Hatteras premiered the 41 Double Cabin, the first fiberglass motor yacht and the precursor of its cruising yacht line. Additional sportfishing models quickly followed. From the beginning, the Hatteras boats were noted for ruggedness, high performance, and extreme comfort.

The market for bigger boats was on the increase, and Hatteras was happy to oblige. Size gradually increased over the years and today the company produces 86 foot convertibles. Hatteras also began

designing and producing a line of cruising yachts that presently range between 63 and 100 feet in length. All Hatteras boats have a solid fiberglass hull bottom with no coring, and are warranted for five years.

In 1967 Hatteras added a second manufacturing facility in the coastal town of New Bern, North Carolina. Thirty years later, the original facility was closed and all manufacturing was consolidated at the 95 acre waterfront site in New Bern, where operations remain today.

The Products

For cruisers: The ultimate cruising experience for those who want only the very best is what the Hatteras 100 Motor Yacht is all about.

Entertainment amenities in the richly wooded salon include a 42" plasma TV, stereo/CD sound equipment, DVD player, and a sunken granite topped wet bar with icemaker and refrigerator. The formal dining area includes a two pedestal dining table with glass or wood top and eight matching dining chairs. The aft deck, equipped with lounge seating, stereo speakers and overhead lighting, allows luxurious al fresco entertainment. Air conditioning throughout offers comfort even on the hottest days.

Downstairs, arched double entry doors lead to the elegant full beam master stateroom, with its king size berth, walk in cedar lined hanging lockers, handsome wood paneling, built in dressers, 32"

plasma TV with CD/DVD player, and five disc changer. The head boasts finished wood cabinetry, marble/granite countertops, a tub with whirlpool jets, and his/her vanities.

And there's still more, including a pilothouse and flybridge (each outfitted with state of the art technology), a fully equipped galley, a coffee bar, laundry room, an owner's office, luxurious guest staterooms, and quarters for a captain and two crew.

For sportfishers: The Hatteras 86 Convertible is one of the world's largest semi custom sportfishing vessels, providing luxurious long range cruising to, and uncompromising tournament fishing in, almost any location in the world. Deep gear ratios allow the large propellers to turn slowly, thereby minimizing vibration, increasing fuel efficiency, and providing constant speed under variable load conditions—all of which results in a quiet, stable ride.

Standard features include two recessed front loading refrigerator/freezer units, a molded in transom fish box, live baitwell circulating system with pump, and a refrigerated fish box (130") with macerator pump. Saltwater and freshwater washdowns, a sink with bait prep area, and ample storage cabinets

complete this awesome 214 square feet of space.

Despite its utility, the 86 Convertible is luxurious and comfortable. The spacious aft deck and expansive salon make for excellent entertaining and dining. Hand crafted cabinetry, bullnose moldings and fluted wood cornices are not only handsome, they cleverly disburse air conditioning throughout the salon and galley. The salon also features a wet bar and high tech entertainment center.

A fully equipped galley, full beam master suite with a king size berth, master head with marble or granite countertops and flooring, three well appointed guest staterooms, a built in bar with wraparound seating, crew's quarters, and countless other touches attest to the excellence of the Hatteras 86 Convertible.

Bellagio

Introduction

In 1998, when the $1.6 billion Bellagio Hotel opened in Las Vegas, it was proclaimed worldwide as the very essence of luxury. The hotel's magnificent trappings extend into the Casino, now considered one of the world's finest.

The Company

Originally envisioned and created by Las Vegas entrepreneur Steve Wynn, the Bellagio has been owned by MGM Mirage since 2000.

One of the world's leading hotel and gaming companies, MGM Mirage owns and operates 24 properties in Nevada, Mississippi, and Michigan, and has investments in four other properties in Nevada, New Jersey, Illinois, and the United Kingdom. Each of these destinations has won praise for its combination of quality entertainment, luxurious facilities, and exceptional customer service.

The company's other interests include the upcoming Project CityCenter, a multi billion dollar mixed use development in the heart of Las Vegas. It also has a 50 percent interest in MGM Grand Macau. MGM Mirage has received numerous awards for its industry leading Diversity Initiative and its community philanthropy programs.

The Place

The 100,000 square foot Bellagio Casino resides in what many people consider to be the world's most jaw droppingly beautiful hotel. Custom draped canopies and coffered ceilings add dramatic touches to the casino.

enjoy privacy while still being part of the casino's exciting action.

The elegance and modernity of the 7,000 square foot poker room is a fit backdrop for one of today's most popular "sports." A Murano hand blown glass chandelier reigns overhead, while intricate marble flooring paves the entryway. Poker artwork graces the walls. The poker room features

40 tables of continuous action. Big play can be had in the two table high limit Bobby's Room, named for 1978 World Series Poker Champion Bobby Baldwin. In addition, a five table high limit area is set off from the main poker room.

But not all visitors enter the casino for such serious action. Many come for a bit of light hearted play, or just to try a few

Club Privé, a high limit lounge and gaming area, opened in 2005. The lounge, with its Art Deco overtones, has an elevated floor that seems to enhance the room's exclusive nature. The lighting is unique and understated, created by Venetian glass panels and chandeliers. Silver leafed screen partitions, set against metal, dark wood, and glass, create a semi enclosed area where players

slots while ogling the opulent backdrop. Whatever reason applies, a top notch array of table games and nearly 3000 slot machines await.

If the luck of the draw and strategic thinking are your game, indulge in blackjack. If you prefer to choose your own lucky numbers, opt for roulette. Other table game classics include craps, Caribbean Stud, Let it Ride Stud Poker, Pai Gow Poker, Big Six, Three Card Poker, and Baccarat.

Anyone joining the Players Club qualifies for benefits, rewards, and special promotions and events. Bellagio adheres to the American Gaming Association (AGA) Code of Conduct for Responsible Gaming.

Cristal

Introduction

For many people, champagne is a splurge—something to imbibe at weddings, anniversaries, birthdays, and other special occasions. For others, the bubbly is simply another wine to grace life's everyday moments. No matter which approach one takes, Champagne Louis Roederer is one of the world's finest champagnes, fit to toast life's most special or everyday moments.

The Company

Based in the Champagne region of France, Louis Roederer was founded in 1776. From its inception Roederer champagnes were popular with the world's titled and wealthy.

One hundred years after the company's founding, Louis Roederer II introduced the now iconic "Cristal" at the special request of Russian Tsar Alexander II. The Tsar, who considered himself to be a connoisseur of champagnes, wanted to serve a bubbly that was noticeably different from that served at other European courts.

The new champagne filled the bill. The Tsar liked it so much that he declared Louis Roederer to be the official champagne supplier to the Russian Imperial Court. Roederer subsequently commissioned a master glassmaker to design a distinctive, flat bottomed crystal bottle for the champagne—hence the name, Cristal.

The Product

Roederer produces a range of champagnes, starting with a basic non vintage and moving up to vintage champagnes. Reigning at the top of all the champagnes is Cristal, one of the world's prestige cuvées, and the central jewel in Champagne Louis Roederer's crown. As one prestigious wine expert put it, "Champagne doesn't get much better than Cristal; in the great vintages, it has no peer."

All Cristal wines are produced from Roederer's own vineyards. A 55 percent Pinot Noir/45 percent Chardonnay blend, Cristal is aged for five years on the lees in French oak barrels. It is then aged six more months after disgorgement.

Cristal is produced with the kind of winemaking standards that require a rigorous selection of crus, vintages, grapes, and wine. Each vintage contains its own magic, but overall you expect a wine rich with ripe fruit, a round attack on the palate—yet, for all that, delicate and fresh. The finish is long, crisp and unforgettable, with a bouquet at once youthful and mature.

Some might prefer the Cristal Rosé—the rarest champagne produced by Champagne Louis Roederer. The traditional skin maceration is used to gently extract the natural pigments for the unique color of this rosé. The grapes used are Pinot Noir from very old vines in the Cumières region of France; they are extremely ripe grapes with outstanding

aromatic concentration. The hallmarks of a great Cristal Rosé encompass a harmonious, enduring palate—fruity but rounded, delicate but powerful.

Aside from Cristal, Roederer produces Brut Premier, its flagship multi vintage Champagne; Brut Vintage; Blanc de Blancs; and Brut Rose Champagne.

Wedgwood

Introduction

Founded in 1759 upon the highest standards of design, craftsmanship, quality and innovation, Wedgwood has been recognized for centuries as one of the world's finest china companies.

The Company

Josiah Wedgwood was born in 1730 in Staffordshire, England, to a father who worked at the local Churchyard Pottery. As a young man, Josiah so excelled as a potter's apprentice that, upon completion of his training in 1754, he was taken as a partner by the renowned Thomas Whieldon (the greatest English potter of his time).

In 1759, at age 30, Josiah founded the Wedgwood Company. By 1766 he had done well enough to build a new factory.

Josiah was known for innovation in all aspects of his work. During his lifetime he invented and produced three of the world's most famous ceramic "bodies."

First, in 1762, he developed a unique cream colored earthenware that so pleased England's Queen Charlotte that she gave permission for the earthenware to be dubbed "Queen's Ware." In 1768 came Black Basalt, an elegant refinement of the crude "Egyptian black" wares of the day. Black Basalt is still used today for relief plaques, busts, medallions, vases, and cameos.

By far the most famous of all Wedgwood's innovations was Jasperware (1774)—the

In 1986, the Wedgwood group became a division of Waterford Wedgwood, whose products have garnered eleven Queen's Awards for export achievement. Waterford Wedgwood is now the largest tabletop manufacturer worldwide. The company's main sales markets today include the UK, Japan, and America.

The Products

Quintessentially British, Wedgwood designs are widely acknowledged

triumphant conclusion to thousands of experiments. Jasperware is unglazed vitreous fine stoneware that can be stained blue, green, lilac, yellow or black to provide a suitable background for white classic inspired reliefs or portraits. To this day, Jasperware is still recognized around the world as the Wedgwood "signature."

Josiah Wedgwood died in 1795, but the Wedgwood name and heritage lives on. In the 1930s, the fifth Josiah Wedgwood purchased 382 acres in Barleston and built a modern all electric Wedgwood factory. The factory has since expanded to four times its original size and is the British pottery industry's most up to date factory.

as timeless, elegant, classic, and understated. The Wedgwood design teams also work with external designers for cross pollination of ideas and experience. Recently fashion designers Vera Wang and Jasper Conran, as well as artist Robert Dawson, left their talented imprint on Wedgwood products, with dozens of new china designs guaranteed to please all tastes.

Shagreen Fine Bone China is a simple classic that can go the long distance as the years pass. With a sophisticated platinum banded pattern and a strong geometric quadrant design, the Shagreen collection artfully combines a modern sensibility with classic beauty. Its raised tone on tone texture is pleasing to the touch; the wide border reminiscent of fine pearls.

Still formal but a bit spicier is the Vera Wang Blanc Sur Blanc Fine Bone China. Simple, elegant, and refined, this collection can be dressed up or down to suit the occasion.

And for those who want to make a bold statement in their formality, there is Jasper Conran's Chinoiserie Green Fine Bone China. With a luscious green background, this collection features an exotic design of graceful birds and delicate flora and fauna.

Wedgwood's casual collections run the gamut from elegant to whimsical. A new addition is Painted Garden China, Forsythia. Reminiscent of an English yard in full bloom, this collection will transport vibrant blooms to the table even in the dead of winter.

La Maison du Chocolat

Introduction

La Maison du Chocolat has transformed the creation and tasting of its chocolates into an exquisite art form. Customers are encouraged to approach each chocolate like a fine wine, tasting for specific flavors and singling out particular aromas. Each variety of chocolate has a name, a history, an ingredient list, and most draw their existence from the inspiration of poetry, dance, or drama. Eating such chocolate is a grand adventure.

The Company

The creator of La Maison du Chocolat, chocolatier Robert Linxe, hails from the Basque region between France and Spain. In 1955, after an apprenticeship in Bayonne, he settled in Paris and opened an upscale food shop, the Marquise de Presles, establishing an immediate reputation as a gourmet and creator of chocolate delicacies.

In 1977 he opened a store devoted only to chocolate—the first Maison du Chocolat (rue du Faubourg Saint Honoré in Paris). This was quite a bold move, since, at the time, Parisians ate chocolate rarely, usually on holidays such as Christmas and Easter. However, Maison du Chocolat was a success, quickly setting a benchmark for combining subtle and unusual natural flavors with chocolate from different world regions.

In 1987, a second Maison du Chocolat was opened in Paris. Today there are five Maison du Chocolats in Paris, two in New York City, and one each in London

For instance, the Sylvia is made of plain milk ganache with a particularly fine coating that allows the center's character and intensity to be fully appreciated; Sylvia was inspired by Linxe's remembrance of

The Product

and Tokyo. The enterprise employs 150 people worldwide, with 50 devoted solely to production.

Helping people learn about chocolate plays a big role for Maison du Chocolat. In New York and London, three different "Parcours Initiatique" classes are designed to awaken chocolate taste buds and sensibilities. The Tamanaco class takes students on a round the world chocolate journey. Andalousie focuses on chocolate and pastries, and The Duo—in association with La Maison des Trois Thés in Paris and Café la Colombe in New York—delves into chocolate, tea, and coffee.

Maison du Chocolat travels the world in search of the finest ingredients, using cocoa beans from Central America, Trinidad, Ecuador, Venezuela, and, to a lesser degree, from Madagascar, Sri Lanka, Indonesia, Sumatra, and the Ivory Coast. Beans from different origins are blended to produce a desired taste. All chocolate is made in a production facility outside Paris—the same location where products are created and tested.

Chocoholics will make a beeline for the ultimate Maison du Chocolat experience, the 3.41 pound Boîte Maison. This elegant, gold lined box contains 33 different and distinct varieties of the company's chocolates.

a ballet by Leo Delibes, "a lively music with a very marked, almost staccato rhythm." The intoxicating, dark center Bacchus contains raisins flamed with rum (the raisins, from Smyrna, are washed, soaked, topped, and tailed before being flamed with a lid placed over the pan so that alcohol vapor fully impregnates the raisins and doesn't risk making the ganache bitter).

Or perhaps the .34 pound Coffret Initiation, containing a selection of the 20 most celebrated chocolates, is a good place

to start. The chocolates are presented in the correct order of tasting, providing an accurate initiation in aroma, taste, and other chocolate sensations. You'll find the Zagora (flavored with an infusion of fresh mint), the Mont Blanc (mousse flavored with kirsch), the Quito (semi bitter, it's composed of beans from very pure growths and has exceptional aroma and fine length in the mouth), and the Faust (spiced with old flamed rum, it's named for the legendary hero of Gounod's opera, whose Walpurgisnacht ballet Linxe considers to be particularly inspiring).

La Maison du Chocolat has also created simple chocolate bars with different cocoa strengths, suitable for eating or cooking: Coro (100%), Cuana (73%), Maracaïbo (57%).

Hennessy Cognac

Introduction

Cognac, a type of brandy produced in the region surrounding the French town of Cognac, is considered to be the finest of all spirits. To be a legitimate Cognac, the wine to be distilled must be made from at least 90 percent Ugni Blanc, Folle Blanche, or Colombard grapes. In addition, the wine must be distilled twice in copper pot stills and aged at least 2.5 years in oak barrels.

The Company

In 1765, Irishman Richard Hennessy was rewarded for his mercenary service to the French King with land in the town of Cognac in the French region of Charante (Cognac was then known as a shipper of salt and wine). Hennessy began a trading business in which he shipped liquor to Ireland, and later, the fledgling United States. In ensuing years Hennessy's son changed the company name to Jas Hennessy & Co.—the name it bears today.

The company has been managed by successive generations of Hennessys, but over the years ownership has changed. In 1971 Hennessy merged with Moët et Chandon. In 1987 the drinks group then merged with fashion house Louis Vuitton to create what is now the world's largest luxury goods business: LVMH (Louis Vuitton Moët Hennessy). Hennessy currently sells about three million cases of cognac each year.

copper pot still again, thus creating a "burnt wine" which was stored in oak barrels. Upon arrival at its destination, the wine was to be diluted. However, some merchants felt that the distilled wine had improved through aging and contact with the wood.

The name "cognac" was first used for distilled wine about 1783. Around the same time, the French government developed rules for labeling, classifying the cognac by it smoothness: V.S. (Very Superior) is aged at least 2.5 years. V.S.O.P. (Very Superior Old Pale), or

The Product

In the 1600s, wines shipped from the town of Cognac were particularly popular with Dutch and English merchants. In order to ensure that the wines made the long journey from France and arrived in reasonable shape, the merchants had the wine distilled in France prior to shipping.

This distillation process involved heating the wine and returning it through the

Reserve, is aged in wood at least 4 years. X.O. (Extra Old, Napoleon, or Extra) is aged for a minimum of 5 years. The final product is diluted to 40 percent alcohol content, or 80 proof.

When celebrating life with a cognac, many people choose the best—Hennessy. Raise a glass to the light and give in to the superb pleasure of the moment.

Hennessy's X.O. (Extra Old or Hors d'âge) is at least 6.5 years old. Originally created in 1870 by Maurice Hennessy using very old eaux de vie, X.O. was reserved exclusively for his family and friends. X.O. has always embodied the finest traditions of Hennessy cognac. Today X. O. is blended from more than 100 eaux de vie, each specially selected from the four premier growing areas (some eaux de vie used in the blend has been aging in the Hennessy warehouses since the early years of the 20th Century).

Rich, full bodied and complex, X.O. combines the spicy aromas of oak and leather with the sweeter essences of flowers and ripe fruit. Well balanced, the initial flourish is dominated by the powerful suggestion of pepper and rancio, which testify to the long years it has spent being aged. Complex. Long lasting. Exquisite.

Alienware

Introduction

Based in Miami Florida, Alienware manufactures high performance desktop, notebook, media center, and professional systems. Alienware computers are specialized for video editing, audio editing, and especially for gaming.

Earning numerous awards for excellence, Alienware has become a respected worldwide brand. For those who demand high performance, superior build quality, innovative style, and award winning support, Alienware is the definitive solution.

The Company

Founded in 1996 by its current CEO, Nelson Gonzalez, and President, Alex Aguila, the Alienware name reflects the founders' fondness for the then popular television series, The X Files. Various product names—Area 51 and MJ 12, for example—also reflect these origins.

At the outset, Alienware was intended to tap a niche in the high performance game market, which, in those days, didn't interest major PC manufacturers. High end game hardware was not widely distributed, so Alienware's founders formed an OEM that sold

frame combine with dramatic highlights, culminating in a truly unforgettable look. Clean lines compose its distinctive silhouette and front air intakes with a low slung grille infuse an aggressive, biomechanical element.

Alienware desktops also provide maximum system security. A single key grants access to independent entry points to enable multiple levels of

personal computers with the highest performing hardware and settings set to benchmarks.

Alienware's explosive growth has them at the threshold of $200 million in annual sales while expanding internationally. So attractive is this company's performance, Dell Computer recently agreed to purchase Alienware. The company will continue to operate under its own brand name.

The Products

The ALX series—state of the art PCs with innovations like silent liquid cooling and performance enhanced hardware—rest at the pinnacle of Alienware desktop systems.

To begin with, these machines are beautiful. Alienware's designs have been described as exotic—even radical. Subtle contours in a heavy duty steel sub security. The user can prevent access to system drives (thus protecting project critical information), secure power and reset switches to avoid inadvertent shutdowns, and prohibit unauthorized access to internal system components.

Consider an Aurora ALX configured for graphics excellence. Equipped with an astonishing four NVIDIA GPUs and backed by Chilled Quad SLI (enabling four graphics cards to work in tandem) and an exclusive Liquid Chilled solution,

it's unmatched for gaming experience—run your most demanding games at ultra high resolutions up to 2560x1600 and at the smoothest frame rates possible. Other features include an AMD Athlon™ 64 FX 60+ Processor, Microsoft Windows XP Media Center Edition, 1GB Low Latency Dual Channel DDR, 250GB 7,200 RPM SATA II w/ 8MB Cache, Quad NVIDIA GeForce™ 7900 GTX 512MB DDR3, and High Performance 7.1.

And then there's the Aurora ALX with crossfire based power. It's loaded with the dual graphics technology of ATI CrossFire and the dual core power of the AMD FX 60 and X2 for incredible performance.

In the world of the laptop, the Aurora m9700 has no challengers. It's the first and only 17" dual graphics card system that gives up to a 100% increase in graphics performance over single graphics card systems. The m9700 possesses the power to pump out games at the highest resolutions without butchering the frame rate. It contains two hard drives, permitting blazing loading speeds and double the space to record up

to 125 hours of television programming with RAID 0 or the impenetrable defense of the mirrored settings and enhanced data backup of RAID 1. And it's backed by the powerful AMD 64 bit Turion processor with HyperTransport technology, allowing lightning fast multitasking. In addition, the m9700 also has S Video In and Out, allowing easy video capture, and a TV tuner to watch favorite programs when traveling.

Le Creuset

Introduction

Le Creuset—the world's leading manufacturer of enameled cast iron cookware—has been the mainstay of French chefs as long as anyone can remember. The skilled craftsmen at Le Creuset have perfected enameled cast iron cookware. Each shape is one of a kind, made from molten steel and cast in a unique mold, and then expertly enameled. No other procedure yields cookware that so evenly distributes heat, browns and caramelizes food to perfection, and creates a masterpiece at the table.

The Company

Based in Fresnoy le Grand in Northern France, Le Creuset was founded in 1925. From the start, utensils were produced by hand casted, molten cast iron in sand molds. Even today this remains the most difficult and delicate stage in the production process. After casting, each mold is destroyed. Every piece of cookware is polished and sanded by hand, and then scrutinized for imperfections. Once the cookware is declared "good to go" for the enameling process, the items are sprayed with two separate coats of enamel. After each spraying, the piece is fired at a temperature of 800°C, resulting in cookware that is extremely hard and durable.

Over many decades Le Creuset gained a reputation for the beauty, reliability, and utility of its products. In 1988, a new management team led by Paul Van Zuydam set out to increase the company's visibility. The result: Le Creuset has been transformed from a relatively small company to a brand recognized worldwide for its masterful blend of fashion, utility, and durability in the kitchen.

The management team has introduced many successful new products as well,

including the Screwpull brand of wine accessories, earthenware, Bijou bakeware, and kitchen textiles.

The Products

All Le Creuset cookware is made from enameled cast iron and, since much of the finishing is done by hand, each piece is completely unique. Adding to its individuality is the wide range of distinctive colors from which the cook can chose, including the signature Flame, as well as Dune, Cobalt, Satin, and others. Highly attractive, each piece of Le Creuset can be used to serve right at the table.

Le Creuset cookware is heavy, but the weight is—and should be seen as—a great strength and a real advantage for cooking. For example, you will never see a Le Creuset pan "dancing" on the stovetop. The wall thickness of a Le Creuset pot or pan, the thinnest and lightest cast iron available, allows even heat distribution and excellent heat retention; the former prevents hot spots, and the latter keeps food warm when serving. Cast iron always maintains its shape and a safe, steady, flat base; the well fitting lids retain

moisture and flavor. Without this solid construction, the pots couldn't withstand the rigors of high temperature cooking such as searing, boiling, and grilling or offer such durability and longevity.

The range of Le Creuset cookware includes Round Ovens, Oval Ovens/Soup Pots,

Buffet Casseroles, Saucepans, Skillets, Grills, Roasters, and various specialty pieces. To illustrate the versatility of all the cookware, consider just one example: the Round Oven. The core piece in a well equipped kitchen, Le Creuset's Round Oven moves with no problem from the refrigerator to the oven or stovetop and onto the table. It can be used for a wide variety of recipes, from savory rice to roast chicken and even to a mouth watering cake. Round Ovens, which come in 2 to 13 quart sizes, can be used for such cooking tasks as simmering, marinating, poaching, braising, and browning. How wonderful that something so versatile and useful has so much panache.

A newer product, the 7 ¼ quart Oval Doufeu, bastes food while it cooks, giving it a taste and tenderness that is unparalleled. With this clever but simple design, the lid's top cradles ice cubes, and, as condensation forms, tiny dimples on the underside evenly baste the roasting meat or poultry. This innovative technology will transform even a mundane cook into a Julia Child.

Crystal Cruises

Introduction

Over the last decade, readers of *Condé Nast Traveler* and *Travel & Leisure* have consistently awarded Crystal Cruises with the industry's most coveted ranking: World's Best Large Ship Cruise Line. Why? It's known as "the Crystal Difference"—an absolute commitment to provide guests with the finest travel experience available in the luxury service market.

The Company

Crystal Cruises is owned by Nippon Yusen Kaisha (NYK), one of the largest and most successful shipping companies in the world. Headquartered in Tokyo, the firm operates over 800 ocean going cargo ships, and has offices around the globe.

In 1986, just after its centennial anniversary, NYK announced that it would expand cruise ship operations and begin a luxury cruise line. Two years later, Crystal Cruises came into existence. Subsequently, the gleaming, all white 940 guest, 50,000 ton Crystal Harmony entered service in 1990. The Crystal Symphony was launched in 1995; and the 1,080 guest Crystal Serenity was introduced in 2003.

Headquartered in Los Angeles, Crystal Cruises is headed by President Gregg Michel, who has been with the line since its inception in 1988. (Michel was appointed president in 2001).

The Product

The company's modern standard of luxury is often compared to the world's finest land based hotels. First and foremost, however, luxury Crystal style is neither stuffy nor intimidating. It represents the very best personal experience a cruise can deliver, from experienced captains, officers, and staff to crew and shoreside personnel who genuinely look forward to welcoming guests into the Crystal Family.

Crystal Cruises' ultra luxurious Crystal Symphony and Crystal Serenity sail throughout the world. The Crystal experience means attention to detail and an availability of choices unsurpassed in the world of travel. It is reflected in a feeling of spaciousness and the highest quality furnishings throughout.

Through its uncompromising focus on classic service, extensive choices and quality, Crystal Cruises has redefined the luxury vacation. As a result, it has become the benchmark against which guests and travel agents now measure all other cruise lines.

Both Crystal Symphony and Crystal Serenity have the highest per guest space ratios of any ships in their class. Private verandahs are available in half of all staterooms on Crystal Symphony and 85% of staterooms on Crystal Serenity.

Crystal Cruises boasts the highest percentage of professional chefs in the large luxury cruise market, and the cuisine is a never ending wonder. The international, contemporary cuisine reflects current culinary trends—but guests can always get an exquisitely grilled steak or lobster. Alternative restaurants offer Asian or Italian dishes. There is also a large assortment of specialty foods such as Russian caviar, gravlax, foie gras, dungeness crab, prosciutto di Parma, and imported cheeses.

An extensive wine cellar dispenses an array of wines from around the world, and premium brand spirits are poured from the well.

Thirty four of the cruise line's 63 global itineraries feature theme programming. Crystal's Big Band and Jazz cruises feature marquee names and hot new talent on Trans Atlantic crossings. Two Film Festival cruises spotlight lectures and film authorities saluting American films. Golf enthusiasts will appreciate the attention from PGA pros and golf celebrities aboard two Golf cruises, affording exclusive

opportunities to tee off at some of the world's legendary courses in the British Isles and Western Europe.

One of the most popular cruises: the Crystal Wine & Food Festival. During this event, some of the most established names in cuisine and wine share the spotlight with the cutting edge stars of the culinary world, providing guests with an experience that is both enriching to the mind and pleasing to the palate.

Lalique

Introduction

Rene Jules Lalique was in Ay, Marne, France in 1860. He was a glass designer, renowned for his stunning creations of perfume bottles, vases, jewelry, chandeliers and clocks. The company he founded is still active today.

The "Lalique" style comes from an artistic gesture, outlining a drawing in total osmosis with crystal, a style one easily recognizes through the richness of the figurative details and the different types of finishing which creates the characteristic contrast of clear and matte crystal. An identity built of softness, femininity and nature with strong Art Nouveau and Art Deco inspirations.

The Company

Recognized as one of the world's greatest glass makers and jewelry designers, Rene Lalique was an imaginative and creative artist in all his work. His early life was spent in many different phases of artistic businesses, acting as apprentice and assistant. This heavily influenced the designs he used in his later life, including his emphasis on glass. He utilized the most modern and innovative manufacturing techniques and equipment available, allowing more than one glass piece to be made at a time while still looking individually hand made. This meant that his quality creations were available to the general public.

Many things influenced Lalique's work, including the natural environment, and the Art Nouveau and Art Deco

and style of the glass creations of Rene Lalique. But in addition to his splendid vases and chandeliers, Lalique was also a great creator of innovative jewelry (his first artistic profession), glass clocks, car mascots (hood ornaments) and perfume bottles.

The Products

Nowhere in all his work in glass is Rene Lalique more renowned than in the vase. His true masterful talent shines in the amber, plum blue, opalescent, gray, green, black and yellow hues he obtained by meticulously adding measured amounts of pigments to darkened glass. Striking animal figures, mythical beasts and geometric shapes poured out from his fertile mind. Lalique's Art Deco style of creating jewelry followed through to his work in glass. Geometric designs, smooth flowing lines and vibrant colors are all characteristic patterns and qualities of Lalique masterpieces.

Lalique collectors are legion around the world. John D. Shearer, a Canadian gemologist and 30 year Lalique collector, said about value: "Prices vary enormously. A small, common and colorless glass vase might sell for $400. Whereas, a large and very rare Art Deco vase can range from $2,000 up to $250,000! Shearer recommends consulting with reputable dealers and reading specialty books before buying for a collection.

periods. The summer holidays spent at Ay, France, and the time he spent at the Syndenham College of Art in London heavily influenced Lalique's naturalistic works. As a result, many of his jewelry pieces and vases showcase plants, flowers and flowing lines.

Glass aficionados and novices the world over marvel at the artistic grace, beauty

Today, Lalique has grown into a solid "lifestyle brand," offering fine jewelry, perfumes, leather and scarves… in addition to the world's most recognized crystal. Whether modern vintage, Art Deco, or antique, the enduring beauty of Lalique is its mystique.

DeBeers

Introduction

Like the source of life itself—light—the radiance that shines from a diamond was born billions of years ago at a time long before mankind's eyes could claim it beautiful. Diamonds are quite simply one of the wonders of the natural world. They possess a fluidity, lightness and rare magical quality that celebrate the 'fire of life'—the intangible essence that fuels our strongest emotions.

Man first discovered diamonds 4,000 years ago in the riverbeds of the Golconda region of India. Today, diamonds are hot and getting hotter. You would expect nothing less from something born beneath a volcano.

The Company

De Beers S.A. is the holding company of the De Beers mining interests around the world. It oversees the De Beers Consolidated Mines in South Africa and The Diamond Trading Company in London, England. They also have mining operations in Canada, Russia, Tanzania, Namibia and Botswana. The company mines more than 45 million carats every year. With expertise in selecting diamonds that spans over a century, De Beers is steeped in diamond tradition and heritage. They are unparalleled anywhere in the world.

It is important to know that every diamond in De Beers diamond jewelry is totally conflict free and child labor free. They are acutely aware of the problem of conflict diamonds and have taken measures to guarantee that no conflict diamonds will ever enter its supply chain or its jewelry.

The Products

Only the finest diamonds are selected to become De Beers diamonds. They are chosen and cut for beauty instead of weight, resulting in a perfect diamond every time. The four most important factors used to measure diamond quality

are cut, color, carat and clarity—commonly known as the 4Cs. This key benchmark standard for evaluating the quality of diamonds was introduced to the world by De Beers back in 1939.

Diamond Beauty is the true standard of any diamond. It is a culmination of brilliance, scintillation, dispersion and symmetry—all maximized through its unique 'cut'. Nature dictates 3 of the 4 Cs with color, clarity and carat. A diamond's true beauty is fully realized in its cut. It is the only factor to be determined by human hand, and at De Beers, they have the finest diamond cutting craftsmen in the world tasked with creating the most beautiful diamond jewelry in the market.

In 2001, De Beers launched a joint venture with French luxury goods company LMVH in order to establish De Beers as a retail brand. This venture has been a raging success. In just a few short years they have opened stores across the globe, including New York, Beverly Hills, London, Paris, Toyko, Osaka and Dubai.

Broyhill

Introduction

For over a century, the name Broyhill has been associated with fine quality furniture making. And, throughout all that time, the guiding force that has defined the company and it products has been a commitment to quality and value. Today, the Broyhill brand is recognized by more than 90 percent of consumers, making it America's best known, full line furniture company.

The Company

Thomas H. Broyhill made his initial investment in furniture manufacturing in 1905 in Lenoir, North Carolina. In 1919, T. H. Broyhill Company became the majority owner of Lenoir Furniture Corporation, manufacturing dining room and bedroom furniture. As early as 1924, Broyhill began marketing its products at the new American Furniture Mart in Chicago. The commitment to aggressive sales and marketing laid the foundation for the company's nationwide recognition as a new leader in the industry.

Broyhill Furniture continued to grow through the early years of the 20th century. In 1926, James Edgar Broyhill, the founder's brother, established the Lenoir Chair Company. This expanded the company's product line into upholstery. Throughout the Great Depression and World War II Broyhill Furniture grew as a result of astute and bold investments in physical facilities,

highly skilled employees and dedicated management. By the 1970s, Broyhill had pioneered the use of assembly line techniques and had become one of the largest and most respected state of the art furniture manufacturing companies in the industry.

In 1980, Interco Inc., a diversified holding company with a stable of consumer goods manufacturers, acquired Broyhill Furniture. Today, Broyhill is part of Furniture Brands International, the world's largest maker of residential furniture.

The Products

Broyhill's extensive product line includes furniture for the dining room, bedroom,

living room, wall systems and home entertainment and the home office. Their numerous couches and sofas come both in upholstery and leather, ranging in style from Traditional, Country Cottage, European American Casual, Contemporary and Eclectic.

The dining room — the very words imply hospitality. A space apart from the hustle and bustle of hectic lives, it is the place to enjoy the good things that come when you gather to dine with family and friends. The three most popular dining options are: the formal dining room, casual dining and the breakfast nook.

The formal dining room is typically adjacent to the living room. Furniture can be of any style, but usually all pieces are from the same look. The table will normally seat eight or more people. A hutch or sideboard takes a place of prime importance for china display and serving.

The casual dining space is usually located between the living room and kitchen areas — conveniently close to both. This multipurpose room is used for dining, homework and hobbies. The furniture should blend stylistically with that of the living area.

The breakfast nook area is typically located at one end of the kitchen or in a custom built bay. The table is sturdy enough to use for dining, hobbies, games and additional kitchen work space. This is the chosen place for the majority of family meals in the fast paced world of today.

Versace

Introduction

Gianni Versace S.p.A is an Italian fashion clothing business founded by Gianni Versace in 1978. It is currently headed by Donatella Versace as creative director and Santo Versace as the Chief Executive Officer.

Versace, today, is one of the world's leading international fashion houses. Versace designs, markets and distributes luxury clothing, accessories, fragrances, makeup and home furnishings under the various brands of the Versace Group.

The Company

Years of designing for the theater earned Gianni Versace a respectable reputation in the fashion industry. However, it was his collaborations with American photographer Richard Avedon that launched Versace onto the stage of the world's elite designers. His 1982 collection introduced metallic garments that would become the trademark, and his elaborate stage costumes for Elton John in the late 1980s helped cement his reputation as one of the beautiful people.

The Versace empire is a family business. Until his tragic death in 1997, Gianni himself held the position of a director of his company. In the beginning, the Versace business tallied roughly $15 million in total sales. Ten years later, this number had risen to $353 million.

The Products

There are several lines which make up the Versace Group. They are Gianni Verace, Versus, Versace Jeans Couture, Versace Ceramic Designs, Versace Collection and Versace Sport. It also operates a hotel, the Palazzo Versace.

Gianni Versace is the main line, which features the high end apparel, jewelry, watches, fragrances, cosmetics and home

furnishings. This is the only line which is presented on the runway during Milan fashion week for both women and men. These amazing designs might cost close to $10,000, and a suit about $5000. Donatella Versace directly oversees this line and designs a majority of the highest end items.

Versace Collection, Versace Jeans Couture and Versus are all licensed diffusion lines. They are clothing lines which take elements of the main Gianni Versace

The introduction of the Versus collection to the New York designer shows in 1995 marked the beginning of an expansion of the North American business for Versace. This move was accompanied by the opening of various new retail stores in America.

line and build on the current seasonal trends. Versace Collection is aimed at a vastly younger audience than the main line, and is also much less expensive. A dress or suit might run about $1000. Versace Jeans Couture is their main casual clothing line. It features high end denim and classic Gianni Versace print shirts. Versace Sport has a more active wear trend and the name is often printed on T shirts that will then sell for around $100.

Versace is favored my many of the world's most famous people. Some celebrities that wear Versace include Elton John, Elizabeth Hurley, Madonna, Demi Moore and Halle Berry.

Napoleon Fireplaces

Introduction

Napoleon – with 500,000+ square feet of manufacturing space and over 400 employees – is North America's largest, privately owned manufacturer of wood and gas fireplaces, free standing stoves, inserts, quality gas and charcoal grills, barbecue accessories, and patio heaters.

The Company

Napoleon Fireplaces began in 1976 when a small steel fabrication business, Wolf Steel, Ltd., was launched by Wolfgang Schroeter in Ontario, Canada. Its purpose: to manufacture steel railings. No one dreamed that the company's successful future would be in fireplaces and gourmet grills.

Yet, a mere three years later the company's first wood stove rolled off the production line. The original stove featured a solid cast iron two door design and was produced in a 1000 square foot manufacturing facility. The name "Napoleon" was born in 1981. At the same time, the first single glass door—the first in the industry—came into being, created from Pyroceram

high temperature ceramic glass and a cast iron frame.

This glass door marked the first of many milestones for Wolf Steel. Over the next few years, the demand for Napoleon wood stoves burgeoned over Canada's borders and into the United States.

Napoleon works with its customers to design and implement the kind of features that consumers really want. The company has repeatedly led the way with innovative, patented technology such as Phazer logs, luxurious Napoleon Gas Grills, and state of the art fireplace technology. Creative engineering and design, advanced manufacturing techniques, dedicated customer service, outstanding product quality, and superior

warranties distinguish Napoleon from its competitors.

The Products

Napoleon's Big Fireplace features a heavy gauge pan burner system that creates a unique Yellow Dancing Flame® with a bright and glowing charcoal bed. It's rated up to 36,000 BTU's, offers a millivolt remote control natural gas valve with built in flame and heat control, and boasts heat transferring, high temperature glass. No electricity is required to light or operate the system (which, by the way, is equipped with a 100% safety shut off valve). Fuel versatility means that owners can choose whether to run the system on economical natural gas or propane.

Many accessories allow owners to design a fireplace to meet specific aesthetic or practical needs. Among these are trim kits in polished brass or brushed stainless steel finish; louvre kits and overlays in painted black, polished brass or brushed stainless steel finish; heritage ornamental insets in painted black, 24 karat gold plated or 24 karat brushed gold plated finish; porcelain reflective panels or metal brick panels; decorative

andirons in painted black or 24 karat gold plated finish; hand held modulating thermostatic remote or digital remote controls; and more.

Many people prefer electric fireplaces, and Napoleon offers a wide range. The Casaloma Electric Fireplace imitates the look of a traditional masonry fireplace. However, this fireplace can be installed almost anywhere. All the owner needs to do is plug it in and enjoy its radiant glow. The fireplace's patented technology

randomly adjusts the flame effect—the height and speed that give the illusion of a wood burning fire. Finely detailed Phazer logs, a pull screen, and the flush design add to the realistic look and feel. These fireplaces come either as a single unit or complete with a cabinet package in either a flush or corner design to suit the décor.

Although it's not a fireplace, Napoleon's Outdoor Cooking Pit offers fun and entertainment. The "campfire style" burner and log set delivers comfort and design in creating a perfect outdoor extension to your home. It easily sets up on your patio or deck surface. It's approved for use on wooden decks, stone or brick patios and concrete, offers all stainless steel construction, is weather resistant, installs easily, runs on natural gas or propane, and will keep guests warm even on the coolest nights.

Bertram

Introduction

Sleek, sophisticated styling and powerful capabilities characterize Bertram sportfishing boats. Drawing from more than 75 years of unrivaled boat building experience and an unceasing pursuit of cutting edge technology, Bertram boats are not only legendary—they're unrivaled.

The Company

Bertram was founded by yachtbroker Richard Bertram. During the 1958 America's Cup Trials in Newport, Rhode Island, Bertram and many others had been intrigued by the extraordinary seaworthiness of a 23 footer serving as tender for a Cup contender. One day, with winds blasting at over 20 knots, the small boat had handily traversed the 6 foot seas.

Designed by Ray Hunt, the boat was named Hunter. Its extreme stability was due to a deep V section running to the stern with a 24 degree deadrise at the transom. Longitudinal strakes gave extra lift, helped throw spray to the sides, and cushioned impact.

Bertram was so impressed by Hunter that he commissioned Hunt to build a 30 foot wooden boat for use at his Miami waterfront home. The new boat—christened Moppie, for Bertram's wife—boasted twin 275 horsepower Lincoln block Interceptors and topped out at 45 mph. Entered in the 1960 Miami Nassau Race, Moppie crossed the finish line nearly three hours ahead of the second boat.

The fiberglass Bertram 31 was introduced in 1961 at a price of $12,000. Orders were so good that, late that year, Bertram

Bertram yet" by Boating Magazine); and many others.

In 1998, Bertram was acquired by Ferretti S.p.A., one of the world's foremost motoryacht manufacturers. Bertram continues to expand its product line and strengthen its position as the world's foremost builder of sportfishing boats.

The Product

The Bertram 670 Convertible belies its sleek and stylish looks with a battleship's performance on the high seas, offering the legendary, wave defying Bertram ride and an exceptionally dry cockpit with none of the spray and mist found in so many other convertibles.

Yacht became a division of the Nautec Corporation, making possible a larger plant, more machinery and a research and development department. In 1962, Bertram opened a 25 acre plant on the Tamiami Canal—the world's first factory specifically designed to manufacture high quality fiberglass yachts. At the end of the first full fiscal year, sales had reached $3.5 million.

Over the years Bertram has introduced groundbreaking boats, including the Bertram 25, one of the most popular models ever; the 38 foot, Deep V design that firmly established Bertram's reputation for fast, dependable, seaworthy sportfishing boats; the innovative 54 foot Bertram convertible; the immensely popular 50 convertible (called "the slickest

salon leads to a full beam master suite with a walk in closet, and a spacious master head with his/her sinks, plus a forward VIP stateroom with in suite head. A starboard twin berth stateroom and portside upper/lower crew's quarters complete the four room plan.

The Bertram 670E offers a luxurious enclosed bridge. This model offers all the same tournament level features as the open bridge 670, including cockpit bait prep center, freezer, live well, fish boxes and trolling valves. No finer bluewater sportfishing convertible is available in the world.

Die hard cockpit amenities are standard: storage for big catches, ample prep area, open sink area, cutting table, live bait storage, and stand up rod storage with a built in washdown shower. From the wheel, a helmsman can see the bow pulpit as easily as the angler fighting a fish in the chair. With Detroit Diesel MTU DDC 2x 1800HP engines, the 670 cruises at 33 knots.

The 670's interior living area layout offers intimacy and space in four distinct areas, all accented with the finest high gloss cherrywood and authentic Italian marble and granite. Aft portside, a living room with couch and armchairs provides seating for 8 10. A complete bar area allows space for barstools. A raised, open galley overlooks the living area and connects directly to the dinette. The

St. Croix Rod Company

Introduction

St. Croix Rod Company aligns the latest advances in technology with time honored handcrafting techniques. The result: some of the finest fishing tools available on the planet.

The Company

St. Croix Rod Company had its beginnings in Unity, Wisconsin, back in 1948, when cofounders and brothers, Bob and Bill Johnson, decided to make and sell landing nets. Constructed of the finest materials and craftsmanship—cedar handles, ash hoops, and hand sewn netting—the resultant nets were justifiably costly. Unfortunately, the nets were too costly for most of their potential customers.

Rather than give up, the brothers started over again. Noticing a display of cane fishing poles, they had a brainstorm: why not modify such poles, making them portable? Cut into three shorter lengths and fitted with brass ferrules, the poles were easy to assemble and convenient for traveling. A local hardware merchant immediately ordered 500 rods, and the St. Croix Rod Company was born.

With brother Doug Johnson and cousin John Olson soon joining the fledgling company, the product line expanded and equipment production improved (an expert machinist, Olson built much of the early equipment). Soon St. Croix opened a second plant in the

nearby community of Loyal. Within the first year the payroll grew from eight employees to 90. In 1954 the company expanded into Park Falls.

Over the years, a variety of goods manufactured were essential to the development and success of the company. Solid and tubular rod blanks were sold to other companies such as Zebco and Waterking. Private brand rods were created for Orvis, L.L. Bean, Cabela's, South Bend, Cortland and many others. Sundry items such as Department of Natural Resources shocking rods and landing nets, pool cues and marine antennas all contributed to the company's longevity.

Today the company is owned by the Schluter family.

The Products

Besides its own technologically advanced rods and reels, St. Croix sells clothing, gear, hats, lures, terminal tackle, line, and many other accessories. Three of many notable products:

St. Croix Legend ice rods feature a patented built in strike indicator system developed by Greg "The Prowler" Wilczynski, a medallist in world ice fishing competitions. The Legend's ultra sensitive spring indicator system, attached to the rod's tip, is built from

durable, high tension stainless steel plated with 24K gold. The indicator allows anglers to see the lightest bump or bite well before actually feeling it. Legend ice rods are available in five models from ultra light to medium heavy. Plus three spring indicators (sold separately) are available in light, medium and medium heavy. Each spring indicator is easily interchangeable; switching from light to medium, for example, is done in just seconds. Every rod can use two different springs to accommodate a large selection of lure weights and styles. Using this unique system, ice anglers will consistently catch fish they would have missed with other types of rods or spring bobbers.

The St. Croix Legend Ultra is the company's most popular fly rod. Its award winning design in high modulus SCIV graphite with ART and IPC technology is graced with slim profile ferrules and top shelf components.

The St. Croix Legend Elite fly rod is made from premium, high modulus, high strain SCV graphite blanks with carbon matte scrim. Then it's outfitted with the finest components featuring St. Croix's stunning slim profile ferrule technology. These rods offer cannon like casting with amazing feel. They are a masterpiece.

West Coast Fishing Club

Introduction

The West Coast Fishing Club was created with the notion of offering guests the most exclusive fishing adventures on the Coast. Business partners Rick Grange and Brian Legge developed the West Coast Fishing Club philosophy almost 20 years ago. Being avid fishermen and owners of a security company based in Toronto, they started inviting their friends and clients alike on corporate fishing adventures. Years of experience fishing on the coast told them that there was no better fishing than the northern Queen Charlotte Islands. Not wanting to fish at locations that offered small, uncomfortable boats, and truly "roughing it" conditions at a fishing lodge, the West Coast Fishing Club was born.

The Company

Two years into their new adventure, Boston Whalers were docked at two prominent lodges on the west coast, providing Rick and Brian's valued guests a touch of class which far exceeded what any other fishing resort company offered. As the Club developed, the next logical step was to build a beautiful, expansive lodge that would meet the same high expectations.

In 1991, The Clubhouse, spanning a full 22,000 square feet, was built on Langara Island, high upon the bluff overlooking the inlet. Its phenomenal success fuelled the desire to build more lodges in other locations in order to offer even more unique fishing experiences in the Northern Queen Charlotte Islands.

to be found anywhere, they will also have the best boats, equipment and fishing guides on the coast. Their location is key to their success—almost all major runs of salmon from the Skeena, Fraser and Columbia River systems must pass by Langara Island during their migration and consequently pass into the fishing grounds of The Clubhouse, the North Island Lodge and The Outpost. This is why the fishing on Langara Island has no equal.

This incredible resort now boasts three unique fishing properties, with others in the works. They have attained and maintained their single commitment to offer the most exclusive salmon fishing experience in western Canada, and possibly the world.

The Places

A visit to one of their B.C. fishing resorts is far more than just a fishing trip. It is a wilderness experience that offers memories that will last a lifetime. The reasons for this are fairly simple— the fishing, location, accommodation, cuisine, service and staff are all world class. Not only will guests be fishing some of the most abundant salmon runs

During the days on the water and back at the lodges, guests find themselves surrounded by breathtaking natural beauty, first class accommodations, gourmet cuisine and personal service that is second to none.

Their Mission Statement: The West Coast Fishing Club is dedicated to offering a world class fishing experience to our members with unsurpassed levels of quality and service, which will be provided by our highly motivated and professional staff, while recognizing our responsibility to our local community and the urgent need to maintain our wilderness resources for future generations.

Their Vision: To be British Columbia's best wilderness fishing resort by consistently exceeding expectations through unparalleled levels of service and quality.

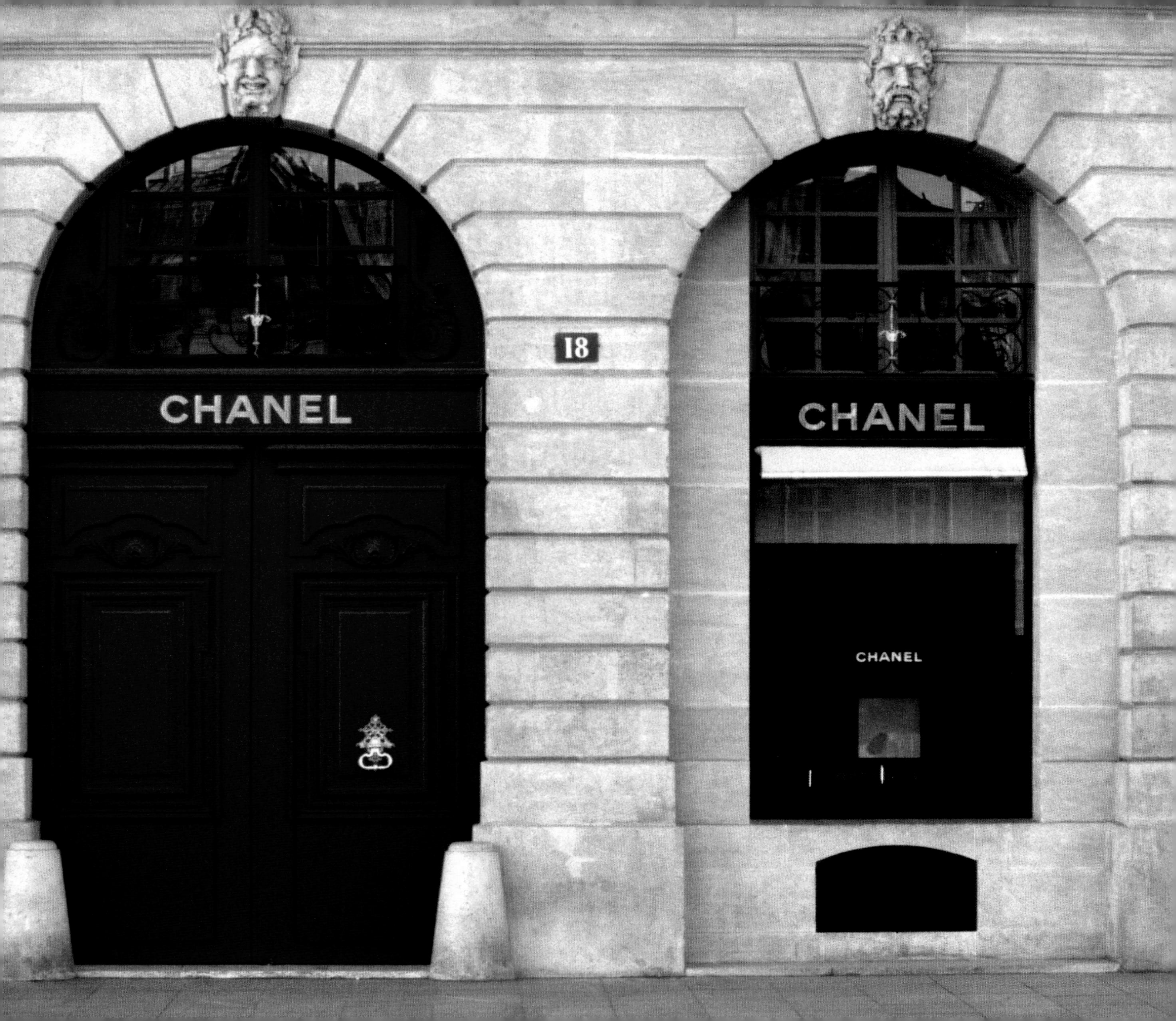
18
CHANEL
CHANEL
CHANEL

Chanel

Introduction

The world's most famous perfume, Chanel No. 5 is still a best seller after more than 85 years. With its blend of ylang ylang and jasmine and its distinctive minimalist packaging, No. 5 remains an indelible symbol of Chanel and the popular culture of the 20th and now the 21st century.

The Company

Although Gabriel "Coco" Chanel died in 1971, she continues to symbolize the company she founded. Born in 1883 in the French provinces, Chanel was a revolutionary couturier who exchanged old fashioned fussiness for modern simplicity in women's clothing. She was so influential in the world of haute couture that she was the only couturier included in Time Magazine's "100 most influential people of the 20th Century."

Chanel started out in 1910 Paris by selling chic women's hats. She did so well that, before the year was out, she moved her business to fashionable rue Cambon and began designing clothing. The "Chanel suit" with a knee length skirt, boxy jacket, and gold buttons, remained popular for decades, and she also made the "little black dress" a must have for women everywhere.

In 1921 Chanel introduced perfume into her lineup. Characteristically, she chose to go against the vogue. Rather than the then popular heavy floral scents in elaborate bottles, she opted for a light, breezy fragrance in a streamlined Art Deco bottle. Chanel referred to it as "a woman's

Toward the end of her life she lived in Switzerland, and is buried in Lausanne.

The House of Chanel in Paris remains one of the world's top couturier houses under famed designer Karl Lagerfeld.

The Products

After the phenomenal success of Chanel No. 5, the company occasionally released other fragrances. These days the lineup also includes cologne and aftershave for men.

fragrance that smells like a woman." Five was her lucky number, so she named the perfume Chanel No. 5. It was the first ever perfume to be sold worldwide, as well as the first to bear a designer's name… and it was a stunning success.

Coco Chanel lived in the Ritz Hotel for 30 years and maintained an apartment atop her couturier shop on rue Cambon.

At the head of the collection is, of course, Chanel No. 5. Worldly, sophisticated, and sexy, this perfume is all about refined seduction. Once, when asked what she wore to bed, Marilyn Monroe replied: "Just a few drops of Chanel No. 5."

Chanel No. 19 was created especially for Coco Chanel and was her personal favorite—for years she and her friends were the only ones privileged to wear it. It's an assertive, intensely feminine perfume with woodsy/floral overtones.

Chanel No. 22, named for the year of its creation, is delicate, romantic, and joyful. Think jasmine, tuberose, and ylang ylang—in gentle doses.

The youthful Chance combines freshness and flowers in a sweet, spicy mixture that seems to say: "Take a chance!" Coco is a mysterious and exciting fragrance, hinting at flowers, wood, and even leather.

Men like the masculine seductiveness and crisp sexiness of Allure Home. Pour Monsieur, developed in 1955, captures the vigor and refinement of polo playing jet setters of the day—the kind of men Chanel knew and loved.

Pebble Beach

Introduction

So compelling is the mystique and beauty surrounding Pebble Beach Golf Links that almost everyone who takes up the game expresses the desire to play here at least once in their lifetime. Few, however, get the chance. With so many claimants and a limited daily number of tee times, most golfers never get to strut their swing on the famous course.

The Company

Pebble Beach Company was founded by Samuel F. B. Morse (a distant cousin of the inventor of Morse Code). In the early 1900s, Morse managed the Pacific Improvement Company, which had extensive real estate holdings on California's Monterey Peninsula. He arranged for the company to build The Lodge and Links, which opened in 1919.

Morse, soon thereafter, formed his own company and bought the 20 acre "Del Monte Unit" from Pacific Improvement Company.

Morse had been determined to build a serious, one of a kind course—one that would be challenging enough to attract major tournaments. He arranged for two amateur golfers, Jack Neville and Douglas Grant, to serve as course designers.

17 Mile Drive—home to The Lone Cypress and other much photographed sights—the emerald fairways rest above the rugged and rocky coast. The course is so stunning that, while playing, most golfers need to constantly fight the temptation to stare westward across endless ocean vistas. Experts say that the course's 543 yard, par 5 18th hole is one of the most beautiful finishing holes in the sport.

Although neither one had any previous experience along these lines, the course they designed stayed mostly unchanged until 1992, when Jack Nicklaus rebuilt the 4th, 5th, and 7th greens to bring them back to their original condition. In 1998 he also designed a replacement 5th hole.

Today Pebble Beach Company owns three resorts and four golf courses. It employs more than 1600 people.

The Place

Few would argue that Pebble Beach is one of the most beautiful courses in the world. Located on California's Monterey Peninsula and poised along the famed

In 2001 Pebble Beach became the first ever public course chosen by Golf Digest as the No.1 Golf Course in America (previously the honor had been given to courses at private clubs).

To date, the U.S. Open has been held at Pebble Beach no less than four times. It will be held here again in 2010. U. S. Open Champions include Jack Nicklaus, Tom Watson, Tom Kite, and Tiger Woods. The 1977 PGA Championship was also held here. Pebble Beach also co hosts the PGA TOUR's AT&T Pebble Beach National Pro Am with two other courses – Poppy Hills and Spyglass Hill. Many other high profile championships have been played on the course, including several U.S. Amateur Championships.

The Homestead

Introduction

Nestled amidst the splendor of Virginia's Allegheny Mountain lies The Homestead, one of Virginia's premier mountain resorts. As one of the country's leading historic resorts and a National Landmark, The Homestead has been providing luxuriously appointed resort accommodations to Presidents, Princes and sports enthusiasts alike since its founding in 1766.

The Company

If there is a place that symbolizes a dynasty in golf, it's The Homestead, because its three courses were all designed by gentlemen who represent the best in golf in their respective genres of time. The Old Course boasts Donald Ross; The Cascades is the work of William S. Flynn; and The Lower Cascades carries the signature of Robert Trent Jones. It's hard to fathom collecting three courses by these legendary architects under one ownership and within minutes of each other, but the Homestead has done it.

All three courses are exceptional, and present different enjoyments and difficulties. The most talked about is the Cascades course. In 2005, this top ranking course underwent an extreme makeover. It focused mainly on the course bunkers. The renovation has restored the Cascades to its original design, as created by William Flynn more than 80 years ago. The majority of the Lower Cascades' holes lie in a beautiful valley, with a few winding up onto the ridges. This course, along with the other two, offer spectacular vistas in every direction.

Over the years, the accolades garnered by this wonderful place are far too numerous to mention. In one year alone—2006—their history of excellence was honored with several Achievement awards. Some of the most notable ones were: The Homestead's Cascades Golf Course named #5 in the "Top 100 Golf Resorts"

The Place

While staying at this luxurious resort guests can choose from over 400 guest rooms.

Many of the 78 suites feature sun porches, working fireplaces and walk in closets. Virtually every room offers splendid views of the surrounding Allegheny Mountains.

Built in 1892, The Homestead Spa is one of America's most historic luxury spas. Still fed by the hot springs that have attracted travelers since the 1700s, this incredible spa offers the ultimate in relaxation and rejuvenation.

Besides their three championship golf courses, the Homestead also features tennis courts, indoor and outdoor naturally heated pools, ski slopes and an Olympic size skating rink. There is also great trout fishing, skeet shooting, and horseback riding.

A stunning selection of dining options is also available here, and range from the formal to very casual. They offer buffet breakfasts, a nice array of lunch dishes, and a tasty four course dinner in the evening. Some of the restaurants include The 1766 Grille, Sam Snead's Tavern, Rubino's Restaurant, The Casino Club and The Dining Room.

in the world (Conde Nast Traveler's reader's poll); The Homestead awarded #15 place in "The Top 50 Spas in North America" (Conde Nast Traveler); and The Homestead ranked one of the "Top 50 Resorts in North America" (Luxury Golf & Travel's annual survey of readers).

Treetops Luxury Lodge & Estate

Introduction

New Zealand is a mythical land steeped in mystery and legend, with a diverse landscape where adventure abounds. Treetops is located in the heart of the trout fishing capital of the world and the famed therapeutic thermal region known as Rotorua. This place is the ultimate in world class luxury accommodation.

The Company

John Sax had a vision to preserve a piece of paradise for people to enjoy generations on end. For more than ten years they toiled, with the planning and planting of habitat, building ponds for trout, controlling predators and laying plans to build a lodge. This was not to be just an ordinary lodge. With his love of nature, he thought perhaps they could build a sanctuary. A place that reflected the very best of what New Zealand had to offer – where one and all could come and appreciate the beauty of nature, become refreshed and depart somewhat enlightened for the experience.

Nestled amidst the magnificent forests and valleys, Treetops Lodge & Estate offers guests a uniquely New Zealand experience. The Lodge was created to embrace the best of the country's pioneering past—elegant architectural style, with timber and stone finishes echoing the beauty and simplicity of the great outdoors.

The Place

This sanctuary and retreat sits on a breathtaking terrain of 2,500 acres of secluded native forest and game reserve. They offer seven trout streams, four lakes, over 70 kilometers of hiking trails, mountain bike riding, horseback riding and the ultimate in tranquility and splendor surrounded by 800 year old forests. Guests can choose from 12 ultra luxurious and unique suites and villas, all with lake and valley vistas.

In keeping with Treetop's eco friendly ethos, a key focus of the fine cuisine that is prepared for their guests is on

locally grown produce. This includes sourcing and utilizing native herbs and ingredients found on the property that were traditionally used by the Maori. Native herbs are not commonly found on the menus of New Zealand, so their gourmet creations provide all guests with a new culinary experience.

Open for only a few years, Treetops is a member of the Small Luxury Hotels of the World and has already received fabulous accolades – from Top New Lodge in the South Pacific (2003 Departures Magazine Reader's Poll) to the 2004 Grand Award winner (Andrew Harpers Hideaway Report).

At the 76th Annual Academy Awards, the Oscar's committee selected Treetops to be included in the Gift Baskets given to celebrity performers and presenters. The committee described this as "the ultimate Oscar gift basket giveaway."

John Sax commented: "It is an honor to be the first New Zealand property accepted for inclusion in the Oscar gift basket. This is a great accolade for Treetops and will further help put New Zealand on the international map with great media publicity both before, during and after the awards ceremony. It is a privilege to be included in what is undoubtedly the most prestigious gala event of the movie world and we look forward to welcoming the stars Down Under. Treetops is a creation of love and passion and I'm delighted that it will be shared by so many people with such fabulous talents."

John Paul Mitchell Systems

Introduction

Back in the late 1970s, two friends had a vision – to found a company by hairdressers for hairdressers – on that would provide tools of success for hair care professionals, their salons, and the entire beauty industry. It all began in 1979, when John Paul DeJoria and Paul Mitchell first decided to launch their professional hair care system around a revolutionary new styling method—hair sculpting, and a new styling product— Hair Sculpting Lotion. By 1980, they had established a partnership with a borrowed $750 which eventually grew to become John Paul Mitchell Systems.

The Company

Initially, the fledgling company faced many challenges. Resources were so limited that the Paul Mitchell brand's now famous black and white packaging was really a result of not being able to afford color ink! At one point, the company consisted of a Post Office box and an answering machine.

However, the partners had a unique and winning strategy—a company building plan that stemmed from their convictions. Mitchell and DeJoria traveled extensively to conduct no cost product demonstrations for salon owners. They guaranteed that all products purchased would sell. Any unsold products would be returned for a full refund. Such practices were a first for the hair care industry, and eventually led to John Paul Mitchell Systems becoming one of the fastest growing privately held companies in American history.

John Paul steers the company according to his original vision. Despite lucrative offers, he refuses to sell the company because of the initial vow he took to be true to the professional beauty industry. Since no public corporation will guarantee that all products stay exclusive to the salons as they are to this day, selling is simply not an option.

The Products

The two partners' dream has flourished. Today, John Paul Mitchell Systems

enjoys retail sales of more than $700 million. The company currently produces over 90 products—including the brands Paul Mitchell, Modern Elixirs, The Tea Tree Collection, and Paul Mitchell Professional Hair Color. All their hair and skin care products are manufactured within the United States. This is a source of great pride for all concerned. John Paul Mitchell System products are sold through 25 distributors within the United States to more than 90,000 hair salons. Internationally, the company works with distributors in an amazing 45 countries to supply thousands upon thousand of hair salons.

John Paul DeJoria strives to make John Paul Mitchell Systems an example for other companies to follow. John Paul states: "Corporations can and should change the world for the better. We have the perspective needed to leave the world a better place for our having been here." This firm commitment to caring for the earth affects every aspect of the company's policy and strategy.

Sound Solutions

Introduction

Sound Solutions was founded in 1977 by David Epstein. Its first incarnation was as a successful music recording studio, producing numerous well known recordings. The company was called upon to design and build residential sound systems of high quality. As home electronics grew increasingly complex, Sound Solutions began manufacturing its own automated home control systems to provide integrated, easy to use touch panel operation of a home's many subsystems.

The Company

As the world of consumer electronics continues to explode—digital, surround sound and High Definition—viewing movies on the big screen at home now offers an experience that surpasses many local movie houses. So it's no wonder many people are incorporating home theaters in new and existing residences. One of the leaders of this burgeoning industry is Sound Solutions, whose work encompasses projects throughout North America. With offices in Culver City, California, Sound Solutions' home turf is the greater Los Angeles area, not coincidentally the major hub for the entertainment industry.

Their client list includes many high profile members of the film, music, media and business communities, as well as Fortune 500 companies in search of the absolute best professional screening rooms, including 35mm film and the latest in DLP video projectors. Many Sound Solutions screening rooms are used by this client base as working

house projects, for instance, the world's largest log cabin (56,000 square feet). Their projects are regularly found on private grounds comprised of multi building estates, presenting challenges that are far beyond those of even very large single homes. Sound Solutions achieves this by applying its expertise and unique methods learned from the commercial field. Imagine a single wall panel, flawlessly controlling security, heating, lighting, pool/spa, water features, security cameras, gates, music

reference systems by which artistic and business decisions are made. The visual images and sound are breathtaking. Often, these systems must co exist in multi purpose rooms, requiring the equipment to cleverly disappear when not in use.

The Products

Sound Solutions has been honored with prestigious national awards including "High End System of the Year", "Best Integrated Home", and "Ultimate Home of the Year." Beyond home theaters, they take on the most challenging whole

and local entertainment systems… and simple enough to be operated by a nanny or house guest.

If it's controllable, Sound Solutions can integrate it. Their projects include homes with live DJ night clubs, performance stage, controlled streams and waterfalls, privacy glass and more. All this is achievable through their trademark blending of art and technology. And best of all, a degree in electronics is not required to operate Sound Solutions' systems.

Sound Solutions people are active on the national stage as recognized industry leaders: on the executive board of directors of Consumer Electronics Association's TechHome division, as panelists, speakers and moderators in demand for industry symposiums and expos, and as authors for national trade publications.

Chateau les Crayeres

Introduction

This incredible chateau was built in 1901. For years the private residence of the Polignac family, Chateau les Crayeres was bought by the Xavier Gardinier family in 1979. Renewed and redecorated, the Castle became a hotel restaurant in 1984. Today, this wonderful property is a member of Relais and Chateaux, a global group of individually owned luxury hotels and restaurants. This elite partnership has over 450 members in 50 countries on all five continents.

The Company

An elegant turn of the XX century residence set in an English style parkland spanning seven hectares, the Chateau les Crayeres blends tradition, comfort and refinement to create a luxurious gourmet retreat where guests can relax in elegant suites and savor superb cuisine. This building that belongs to a previous century has been elegantly decorated by Pierre Yves Rochon.

The accolades accumulated by this unique hotel defy comparison. Some of the awards given to Chateau les Crayeres in the last five years alone include: World's Best Hotel – *Travel and Leisure 2002*; World's First Hotel – *Conde Nast Traveller 2002*; World's Best Small Hotel – *Zagat Guide 2003*; and Chef of the Year awarded to Didier Elena by two different publications.

The Place

Chateau les Crayeres was once owned by Madame Pommery, the lady whose name, in the world of Champagne, rivals that of the old widow Clicquot herself.

Most trees found on the property were actually planted by Madame Pommery. The building is a splendid, cream colored classic chateau design with a slate Mansard roof supporting statues and chimneys sitting atop the two stately wings of the structure. Inside, the halls are graced with portraits of plump, creamy women and be wigged man. The salon sports soaring ceilings and massive chandeliers and the dining room is a masterpiece in turn of the century overstatement—all cherubs, tapestries and gilt.

Set in perfectly manicured gardens with rooms rich in extravagant décor, this Reims castle is surrounded by vineyards, and is home to impeccable service and world renowned kitchens that serve up celebrated Champagne gourmet feasts. Some restaurants have superb cuisine, some hotels are like private palaces and others offer charm and a warm welcome. The restaurant Chateau les Crayeres is a rare combination of all three.

General Manager Fabrice Mercier and Chef Didier Elena have combined forces to create an atmosphere that makes their guests feel like family friends spending time in an elegant home of French nobility. The service at Chateau les Crayeres is unparalleled in the hospitality industry. This comes as no surprise when you realize that 88 employees look after a maximum of 40 guests.

Gulfstream

Introduction

For nearly 50 years, Gulfstream Aerospace Corporation's business jets have been widely acknowledged as the world's most technologically advanced. More than one quarter of Fortune 500 companies operate Gulfstream aircraft.

The Company

Born in 1895 on Long Island, New York, Leroy Grumman witnessed the birth of aviation—which may have accounted for his lifelong fascination with flight. He received an engineering degree from Cornell University in 1916, became a flight instructor with the Navy, and later studied aeronautical engineering at MIT.

In 1930 Grumman started his own company, Grumman Aeronautical Engineering, on Long Island. The company's growth exploded at the beginning of World War II, and soon Grumman became the main source for Navy fighter planes, including the 330 mph F4F Wildcat, the F6F Hellcat, and the TBF Avenger torpedo bomber.

After the war Grumman expanded its interests into civilian aircraft. The first Gulfstream was a twin turboprop, the Grumman Gulfstream I. Later came a business jet, called the Grumman Gulfstream II.

Today the company is owned by General Dynamics.

8C Rolls Royce engines, combined with aerodynamic and material improvements, its flight and performance characteristics provide greater fuel efficiency and lower operating costs.

The Products

The large cabin, ultra long range Gulfstream G550 is the most technically advanced aircraft of the fleet. It's capable of cruising at an altitude of 51,000 feet, and achieves speeds up to Mach .885. Powered by two Rolls Royce engines, the G550 has the longest flying range available in a business jet—6,750 nautical miles.

The G550's cockpit contains the most advanced avionics suite in the industry. Standard equipment includes the Gulfstream Enhanced Vision System and the Gulfstream Signature Cursor Control Devices. The fully equipped G550 offers a choice of cabin layouts and well

planned option packages. Customization packages are also available. Dependent upon the configuration, the G550 can accommodate 14 to 18 passengers.

The Gulfstream G500, also powered by two Rolls Royce engines, flies 5,800 nautical miles with eight passengers at a cruising speed of Mach .80. This plane's required takeoff distance is only 5,150 feet. Multiple cabin layouts and configurations are available.

The Gulfstream G450 offers the ability to accommodate 12 to 16 passengers, travel 4,350 nautical miles and cruise at speeds up to Mach .88. This plane can handle domestic and international flights with equal ease. Powered by upgraded Tay 611

The Gulfstream G350 offers the most cabin volume, the best performance and the largest number of standard features compared to any aircraft in its class. Powered by two Rolls Royce Tay 611 8C engines, the G350 has the ability to accommodate 12 16 passengers, travel at a maximum range of 3,800 nautical miles and cruise at speeds up to Mach .88.

The large cabin, mid range Gulfstream G200 accommodates up to 10 passengers and offers outstanding performance with its excellent climb, high cruising altitude, high speed, long range and short landing capabilities. It is powered by two Pratt & Whitney PW 306A engines, and can fly at speeds up to Mach .85 and at cruising altitudes up to 45,000 feet.

The Universal Aft Galley with C

Tiffany & Co.

Introduction

Tiffany and Company's blue boxes are one of the world's most recognized and valued brands, denoting quality and luxury. When Truman Capote wrote a story in which a madcap single girl in New York City dreams of being rich and famous, he focussed her longing on the company's Fifth Avenue store. The millions who read the story or saw the movie—both entitled Breakfast at Tiffany's—understood exactly what he was getting at.

The Company

In 1837, Charles Lewis Tiffany and John F. Young founded Tiffany & Young on Broadway in New York City. The first day's total sales: $4.98. At first the store sold stationery and costume jewelry, but in 1845 they began selling authentic jewelry and also published their first mail order catalog. They would later add silverware, timepieces, perfumes, and other luxury items.

In 1853, Tiffany bought out his partners, and the store became Tiffany & Co. Tiffany began catering to the growing number of wealthy Americans. When he died in 1902, his son Louis Comfort Tiffany became the company's artistic director. Thanks in large part to his designs, the company's sales reached almost $18 million in 1919.

In 1940 the company moved to its present Fifth Avenue location, and in

1955 the Tiffany heirs sold their shares to Hoving Corporation, which opened stores in San Francisco (1963), Beverly Hills (1964) and Houston (1964). Tiffany's was sold twice more before going public in 1987. Today the store has 30 retail locations worldwide, as well as a strong online presence.

The company is renowned for its customer service, giving new employees approximately two months' training in customer skills and product knowledge.

The Products

Tiffany & Company products cover a wide gamut, including: fine jewelry (diamonds, pearls, colored stones, platinum, gold, and silver); engagement and bridal jewelry; watches and other timepieces; sterling silverware; fine china; crystal; stationery; and perfumes.

However, it is for jewelry that Tiffany is justly famed.

Consider the Cell diamond bracelet. With a total carat weight of 16.63, a color grade of H, and a clarity grade of VS, it's set in platinum and is 7 inches long. Or perhaps you'd prefer the Flower bracelet,

with its round brilliant and pear shaped diamonds, a total carat weight of 11.69, and the same color and clarity grades as the Cell bracelet; set in Platinum, it's 7.25" long. The price for either piece approaches $100,000.

There are so many choices and types of engagement rings that it's almost impossible to choose. Many clients prefer a simple solitaire with the famous Tiffany setting, in which the diamond

is lifted into the light for the utmost in brilliance, dispersion and spectacular scintillation. The three stone rings are meticulously planned to match stones for color, quality, and proportion. Legacy rings are inspired by Edwardian designs, with a cushion set center stone surrounded by bead set diamonds. There are modern, fancy, traditional, and offbeat rings, and the price will always depend upon carat weight, color, clarity grades, and specific design.

Roche Bobois

Introduction

Through the melding of artistic eras, superb designs, and exquisite materials, Roche Bobois creates furniture that expresses a beautiful and elegant approach to luxury living.

The Company

Roche Bobois was founded by two furniture selling families in Paris: the Roches and the Chouchans. For a decade, both families lived in the same city and worked in the same industry – but never met. When they finally did, lightning struck.

In 1950, Jacques Roche began selling furniture on the rue de Lyon. Sometime later he was joined in the business by his two sons, Philippe and François. The company focussed on the best in contemporary furniture inspired by Bauhaus and other modernistic designers.

At around the same time the Chouchan family's store, Au Beau Bois—later shortened to Bobois—was in business on Boulevard Sebastopol. Like the Roches, the Chouchans also concentrated on modern furniture.

In 1960 the families finally met—not in Paris, where they lived and worked, but in Denmark, where all were attending the Copenhagen Furniture Salon. Scandinavian furniture was then entering its vogue, and both families were planning to import it to France. The Roches and the Chouchans hit it off so well that they joined forces, designed a catalog, and launched Roche Bobois as a franchise.

The Products

Roche Bobois offers three signature collections: Les Contemporains, contemporary and sometimes cutting edge; Les Provinciales, a new take on the traditional French furniture; and Les Voyages, inspired by distant cultures.

If you are drawn to Les Contemporains, you might find yourself lounging on the superb Terre de Lune sofa: thick, full grain leather, with a double back and armrest cushions, spring seat suspension,

The following year, 1961, the first nationwide Roche Bobois advertising campaign (in Elle magazine) got the attention of the all important French female furniture buyer. Sales skyrocketed, proving that the combining of names and resources was working.

Today Roche Bobois is one of the most internationally renowned and exclusive brands in home furnishings. With facilities in nearly 30 countries, the company is an established global presence. A new Roche Bobois store opens somewhere in the world each and every month.

a frame made from solid beech and pine, either chromed metal or solid beech legs, and—if you like—a matching armchair and ottoman.

Perhaps Les Voyages is more to your liking. Imagine serving hors d'ouevres on the spectacular Nairobi cocktail table, with its solid bubinga frame and sonokeling Alveoles hand sculpted motif doors with a rosewood stain. Perhaps you'd match it with the wraparound Vera Cruz sofa with its removable Baku slipcover and cushions of down.

Then, too, you may seek tradition with a twist. If so, opt for Les Provinciales and you could find yourself deep into a Haendel sofa—a Louis XV style two seater with an antiqued patina and a hand waxed finish. With comfortable feather and foam cushions, Louis himself never had it so good. Across the room is the solid cherry Hauteville bookcase with its bi color antique patina. Nearby, your favorite reading chair: a Louis XVI style Marie Cécile Marquise made of solid beech with silver lacquer and antiqued patina.

Louis Vuitton

Introduction

Over its long history, Louis Vuitton has come to stand for the highest quality of luggage and other related products. During the production process, any suitcase or handbag that does not meet the company's high standards does not see the light of day.

The Company

In the early 1800s, Louis Vuitton was employed as a packer of luggage for wealthy families. His packing career peaked when he was appointed by Napoleon III to pack Empress Eugenie's dresses. With such a background, he developed definite ideas about trunk design and, in 1854, Vuitton began to manufacture travelers' trunks in Paris. It was a simple start for the founder of what would soon become a world famous dynasty.

Vuitton's early trunks were of such impeccable quality that, in 1860, he opened a larger factory to keep up with the demand. The quality remained high, accounting for the bronze and gold medals won by Vuitton at the 1867 and 1889 World Fairs.

After Louis died in 1892, his son Georges developed the company's famous beige on chestnut monogram of intersecting LV initials. It is considered to be the first ever designer label.

The Pegase Rolling Suitcases offer comfortable leather handles and sturdy, noiseless wheels for easy carting. The Pegase 50, at 14.2 x 20 x 7.1 inches, is sized for overnight trips or short journeys. It opens from the top with a double zipper and has a large outside pocket with a zipped compartment. Inside it offers a spacious zipped pocket and two flaps to keep clothing secure. Some overnight travelers might prefer the slightly larger Pegase 60. The Pegase 70 (16.5 x 27.6 x 9.5 inches) is perfect for longer travels. It offers two inside pockets, as well as a removable hanging suit carrier with a flap pocket.

Non rolling bags in the Pegase line include the Alizé (22 x 17 x 8). With

In the years since, Vuitton has become synonymous with luxury consumer goods. Today the company sells products that include appointment books, perfumes, watches and designer clothing.

The Products

The classic Pegase suitcase line incorporates traditional style and modern convenience. The monogram canvas with natural cowhide trim and golden hardware is reassuringly familiar.

a comfortable shoulder strap and large inside pockets, it's a great carryon bag.

The Carryall is perfect for a low key weekend getaway. Rolled cowhide handles and a securing belt, a textile lining, double zipper closure, lockability, two outside pockets, and protective bottom studs make this a well thought out bag.

For long trips, the Satellite 70 is the preferred choice of many. The slightly expandable sides are securely anchored by sturdy buckles. An inside elastic strap keeps clothing in place. Protective feet and corner pieces help keep the Satellite's integrity intact through the numerous knocks of long travel.

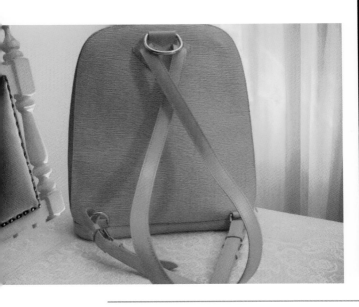

Harley Davidson

Introduction

Mention the word "motorcycle," and the name of Harley Davidson surely comes to mind. For nearly a century the Harley Davidson brand has reigned at the peak of the motorcycle world, representing the finest in technology and quality—and a certain panache that no other motorcycle can match.

The Company

Back around the turn of the 20th Century, the concept of motorcycling was brand new—the pioneering Indian hadn't appeared until 1901. And so, in 1903, when Milwaukee residents Bill Harley and Arthur Davidson began putting together a one cylinder motorcycle powered by a gasoline combustion engine, they were heading into new territory.

The first motor bike they constructed wasn't able to climb the hills, so they immediately drew up plans for a more powerful version. The first "real" Harley Davidson motorcycle, it possessed a 24.74 cubic inch engine (405 cc) with 9 3/4 inch flywheels weighing 28 pounds. Its entry in a September 1904 race marked the first competitive appearance of a Harley Davidson motorcycle.

The duo first sold Harley Davidson engines to do it yourselfers, and then offered complete motorcycles. By 1906 they had a small production company established in an old wooden barn owned and built by Davidson's father. Before long they were at the helm of a thriving enterprise. From the start, First Place winnings in races and other contests brought recognition and hefty sales. At about this time they began selling motorcycles to police departments nationwide, a tradition that continues to this day.

The Products

The Ultra Classic Electra Glide is, in the company's own words, a touring bike "for those who want it all… it's everything you expect a Harley road machine to be." Indeed. Start with the comfort stitched heated leather saddle with a wraparound passenger backrest.

Move on to spacious hardbags and a two position King Tour Pak with LED side lights, heated grips, leather dash, vented fairing to keep legs cool, reduced clutch lever effort, integrated storage, electronic passenger controls, and an advanced audio system by Harman/Kardon. All gracing a powerful Twin Cam 103 with all the trimmings.

For those out for fun, the Sportster's potent engine and agile frame is the choice of many. The Sportster 1200 Custom is a top contender, with its chrome covered 1200cc rubber mounted Evolution engine, its laced front wheel and chrome slotted disc rear wheel, its generous 4.5 gallon tank, low rise handlebars, and electronic speedometer. It also boasts a 2 piston, single disc front and single piston rear brake system. It is small wonder that the Sportster is one of Harley Davidson's most popular bikes.

Harley Davidson's VRSC family of sleek bikes translate to speed. Whether it's the V Rod, the Night Rod, or the Street Rod, the rider thrills to straightaway acceleration. That is thanks to a liquid cooled, fuel injected 60 V Twin Revolution powertrain with

dual overhead cams, four valve heads, two powerful stacks housed in a massive air box and the rigid hydro formed frame. This incredible machine is the most award winning of all Harley Davidson motorcycles.

Featherlite Luxury Coaches

Introduction

A division of Featherlite Coaches, Inc., Featherlite Luxury Coaches manufactures two distinct luxury motorhomes, the Featherlite Vantare H3 45 and the Vantare XL11. Both these phenomenal vehicles are Prevost bus shell conversions that offer the utmost in luxurious living accommodations, interior choices and leading edge technological features.

The Company

Since the mid 1990s, Featherlite has been making luxury coaches at its facilities in Sanford, Florida. They have expanded over the years and now have sales and service centers strategically located throughout the United States. Owners of Featherlite coaches are encouraged to become involved in all aspects of the planning and design of their new custom luxury motorhome. Customers have more than 200 amenities and state of the art options to choose from as they create a truly unique luxury coach designed to accommodate their every comfort.

Some of these amazing options include a 50 inch retractable plasma television, elaborate internal and external entertainment systems, leather seating, brass and etched glass showers and in motion satellite systems. Featherlite also designs and manufacturers coaches in corporate and executive models.

Featherlite has spent the last decade perfecting the art of custom coach

The stateroom features a king bed with a plasma television that lifts out of the footboard. The headboard has mirrored posts with Schonbek crystal and antique bronze leaf sconces. The walls are European Strie and all bath hardware is from France, finished in copper and crystal. The shower walls are onyx.

In the galley, the chef has a highly efficient and stunningly beautiful work space. Amenities include full high cabinets with copper fused glass, pull out pantry, Sub Zero refrigerator freezer and an onyx

manufacturing. Their client list includes Fortune 500 Companies, major league sports organizaions and some of the nation's foremost independent businesses. Featherlite Luxury Coaches is proud to be the "Official Coach" of NASCAR.

The Products

Their newest and most exclusive motor coach edition is the Vantare Platinum Plus. This luxury coach is among the most expensive on the market today, retailing at $2.5 million.

Its spacious interior is defined by the finest grade of finish materials in the world. The entry steps are made of rare Inca marble. The risers are hand made glass tile with imbedded copper. The ceiling and AV cabinet are covered with pearlized Italian leather while the dash and steering wheel are Sapele Pommele from Africa. The helm is equipped with an Avic N 2 global positioning system with real time traffic and weather alerts.

The salon features a custom Italian sofa with double electric recliners. It is upholstered in Correggio fabric. There is also a special liquor cabinet stocked with signed crystal glasses by Michael Weems and a decanter from Neiman Marcus. Ceiling lighting shines through Swarovski crystal.

dining table. The galley and dining area come fully stocked – Haviland Limoges place settings, flatware handmade from South Africa, blown and signed crystal wine glasses, and pots, pans, serving pieces, linens and placemats. This is truly a turn key coach.

In the eyes of many, the Featherlite Vantare Platinum Plus is a luxury coach without equal in the world today.

Thos. Baker

Introduction

Thos. Baker LLC is a privately owned company headquartered just a short ferry ride from downtown, Seattle, Washington on beautiful Bainbridge Island. They are dedicated to bringing the discerning consumer ultra high quality, distinctive garden furniture crafted from plantation grown teak. All their teak is harvested under controlled, sustainable yield practices.

The Company

This highly successful company and its luxury line of products are all about the teak.

Tectona grandis is a deciduous hardwood tree indigenous to the dry, hilly terrains of Indonesia and Southeast Asia. Teak is extremely dense grained and highly resistant to rot, warping, shrinkage and swelling. Its high natural oil content acts as a powerful preservative to the wood, so it can be left outdoors for decades.

The first outdoor teak benches were made of recycled decking from old sailing ships. Amazingly, many public parks in England are furnished with such teak benches, some of which are nearly a century old.

Unlike most of us, teak ages gracefully. Over time it develops a silvery gray patina that can be left in its natural state or revived to a warm honey glow with a light sanding or the application of a little teak oil.

Quality custom made teak outdoor furniture is typically classic in design with clean architectural lines and timeless style. These attributes make Thos. Baker patio furniture one of the best values available in the home furnishings industry.

The Products

Thos. Baker uses only "one side clear" teak heartwood with a mix of straight and free grain. Components are visually matched to a high degree of color uniformity.

There are minimal "live" knots and no dead knots or sap lines. Consumers will never see any wood filler, inserts, gaps, cracks or bowing in their furniture.

Some of the more popular teak furniture collections offered by Thos. Baker are:

Craftsman Deep Seating Outdoor Furniture – it features big beefy cuts of

their premium teak in an iconic mission inspired design. Customers choose extra thick in several rich colors. At home indoors or out, the Craftsman lounging pieces and occasional tables exhibit a clean design and supreme comfort.

Montecito Collection of Teak Patio Furniture – features a contemporary expression of the traditional teak garden furniture vocabulary. The slatwork is narrower than most, highlighting

the precision joinery and detailed workmanship. And the standard brass fittings have been replaced with gleaming stainless for a fresh look with yacht building integrity.

Jimbarian Collection of Deck and Patio Furniture – features traditional forms, premium materials and craftsmanship. This wonderful collection of teak garden furniture has dining tables, folding chairs, recliners and benches that all share a design lineage and practical functionality that has easily stood the test of time.

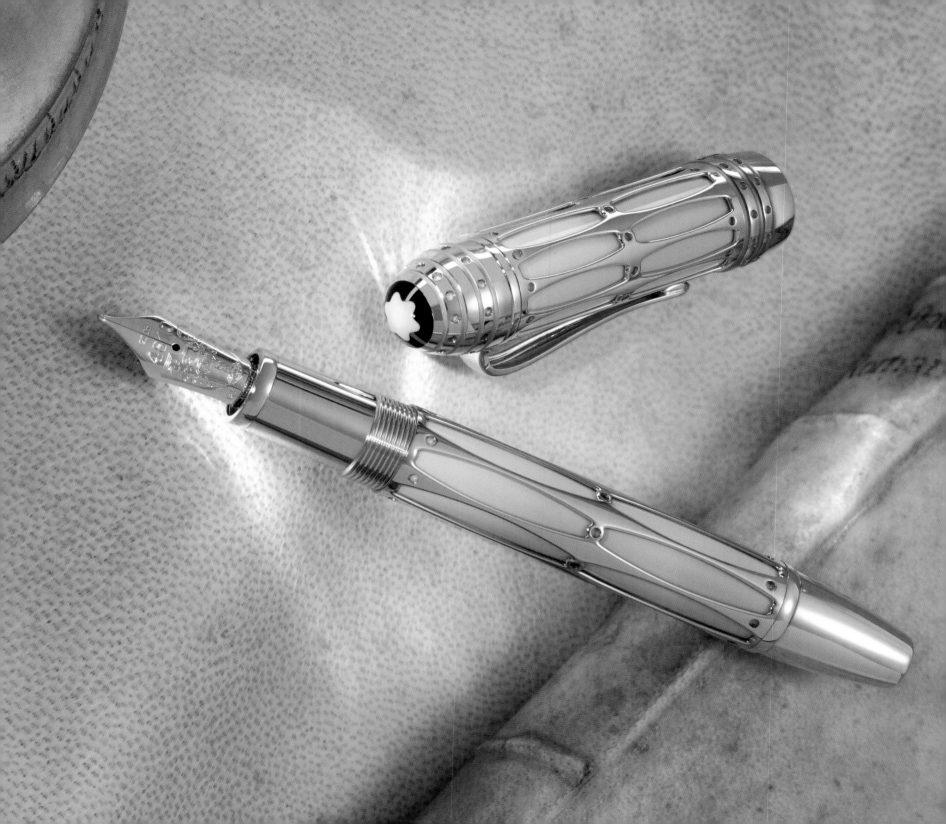

Montblanc

Introduction

The perfection, craftsmanship, and sheer beauty of Montblanc fountain pens have made them the world's most desirable. Writing with a fountain pen gives panache and even character to the written word. Writing with a Montblanc also imparts joy to the writer.

The Company

Montblanc's origins hark back to 1906, when three Germans–Claus Johannes Voss, Christian Lausen, and Wilhelm Dziambor–decided to manufacture high quality fountain pens. Self filling pens had only been produced in the last few years, and the field was ripe for innovation.

Naming their company the Simplo Filler Pen Company, the trio soon introduced the Rouge et Noir fountain pen; it was made from black ebonite rubber and was topped by a red cap.

In 1910 the company's name was changed to Montblanc. According to legend, the founders drew an analogy between Europe's highest mountain,

Today Montblanc is owned by the Richemont Group, a Swiss luxury goods company founded in 1988 by South African billionaire Anton Rupert. Other Richemont companies include Van Cleef & Arpels, Piaget, Baume et Mercier, and Alfred Dunhill, Ltd.

The Products

To celebrate its 100th Anniversary, Montblanc created a trio of special pens that are bound to become valuable collector's items in the years ahead: the Meisterstück Solitaire 100, the Meisterstück Solitaire 1906, and the Starwalker.

The Meisterstück Solitaire 100, limited to one hundred pens, boasts a barrel and cap crafted of solid 750 white gold, an 18K gold nib, and, atop the cap, a patented star cut diamond.

The cap of the Meisterstück Solitaire 1906 (limited to 1,906 pens) is crafted from granite ground out of a Mont Blanc boulder. The barrel is 925 Sterling Silver; the nib 18K gold. Atop the cap: a diamond with 43 facets.

The Starwalker is made of black precious resin with platinum plated rings and clips. The nib is 18K gold. The diamond atop the cap floats in a transparent dome.

Other special edition pens offered by Montblanc include the Greta Garbo, which celebrates the 100th year of the famed star's birth. Modish and sensual in appearance, the pen possesses a black barrel and cream colored cap made of resin, platinum plated fittings, a clip

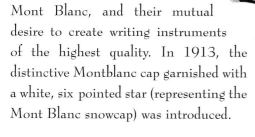

Mont Blanc, and their mutual desire to create writing instruments of the highest quality. In 1913, the distinctive Montblanc cap garnished with a white, six pointed star (representing the Mont Blanc snowcap) was introduced.

Montblanc expanded internationally, but for decades its major market remained in Germany. The company nearly foundered during World War II, but began production again at war's end. An incredible comeback ensued, and by the 1980s, Montblanc was the world's most well known luxury market pen, the iconic equivalent of a Patek Phillipe watch or a Maserati sports car.

set with a white Akhoya pearl, and a platinum plated 18K gold nib with a heartshaped hole.

Other editions honor great writers such as Ernest Hemingway, Agatha Christie, Marcel Proust, and Jules Verne, as well as historic art patrons like Louis XIV, Lorenzo de Medici, and the Marquise de Pompadour. The design and feel of each pen reflects the person who inspired it.

Brunswick Corporation

Introduction

From its inception in the 17th Century, pool has been one of the world's most popular games. For nearly half that time Brunswick has produced the world's finest billiard tables.

The Company

Emigrating from Switzerland to the United States in 1834, young John Brunswick apprenticed as a woodworker in New York City and Philadelphia, and then established his own carriage making company in Cincinnati. Gradually accumulating a reputation for impeccable craftsmanship, Brunswick expanded into cabinets, tables, and chairs. Successful, he might have continued on this way forever but for an unexpected twist of fate.

One night in 1845 he saw a billiard table for the first time and found himself mesmerized by its intricate carving and the beauty of its workmanship. It didn't take him long to decide to change his course in life. In 1845, the J. M. Brunswick Company produced its first billiard table—and by 1850 Brunswick tables were known around the globe as masterpieces of craftwork and design.

The first American celebrity to own a Brunswick table was Abraham Lincoln, a self confessed "billiards addict." Since

Today, headquartered in Lake Forest, Illinois, the Brunswick Corporation is a leading manufacturer and marketer of high quality products for recreational enthusiasts. With more than 26,000 employees, the company generated close to $6 billion in sales last year.

The Products

No matter your taste or decorating style, you'll find a Brunswick table to fit right in. Selections include Arts & Crafts, hard edged Contemporary, Traditional, European, Casual, and more.

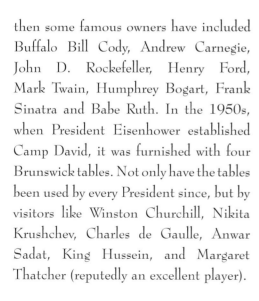

then some famous owners have included Buffalo Bill Cody, Andrew Carnegie, John D. Rockefeller, Henry Ford, Mark Twain, Humphrey Bogart, Frank Sinatra and Babe Ruth. In the 1950s, when President Eisenhower established Camp David, it was furnished with four Brunswick tables. Not only have the tables been used by every President since, but by visitors like Winston Churchill, Nikita Krushchev, Charles de Gaulle, Anwar Sadat, King Hussein, and Margaret Thatcher (reputedly an excellent player).

A top of the line choice might be the 9 foot Cromwell. Infused with a timeless beauty, it expresses the richness of 17th Century European styling. A beautiful walnut finish emphasizes the elegant details and the ornately carved rails, sills, and legs. This is one magnificent piece.

In the Contemporary model, the Manhattan has a bold and edgy style. Sophisticated, sleek, and stunning, it's available in Maple or Black with stainless steel legs and touches.

The Mission table, in the Arts & Crafts collection, is hands down the truest representation of Mission style available in any billiard table. Clean and unornamented with superb lines, this table anchors any room in an elegant manner.

Antique lovers will thrill to the Traditional line, with styles interpreting 17th and 18th Century designs. The Greenbriar shows a classic arched base with Ball & Claw legs (optional legs include Queen Anne, Ram's Head, and Tapered) and an oak, cherry, or mahogany finish.

LRW Club

Introduction

The newest concept in luxury travel, destination clubs offer their members access to upscale residences in multiple locations, for a fraction of the cost of a single vacation home.

When three titans of the travel and leisure industry set out to redefine luxury vacations, they left the competition speechless. The result is the creation of a destination club that sets new standards for the industry: The Leading Residences of the World.

The Company

The Leading Hotels of the World, Ltd., representing the largest collection of elite hotels on earth, and Cendant Corporation, a global leader in travel and real estate, teamed up to create a destination club with an unprecedented array of benefits. The third partner in this alliance, HDMD, comprised the team that launched the world's first private residence club, and continues to introduce more of these successful real estate offerings than any other entity.

The Places

Leading Residences of the World currently has a portfolio of elegant homes, villas and urban residences—ranging in value from $1 million to $5 million—located in prestigious destinations from Cabo San Lucas to Paris, and from Maui, Hawaii to Marbella, Spain. They will soon surpass forty properties in their luxury portfolio.

Carefully selected for quality, on site amenities, and proximity to beaches, golf courses, ski trails or urban attractions,

the homes represent the crème de la crème of vacation real estate. However, the founders of this exclusive club wanted to give their members more than just beautiful places to stay.

"Destination clubs provide exceptional vacation luxury and convenience," observes Paul McManus, president and CEO of The Leading Hotels of the World, Ltd. "To maximize those advantages, we designed Leading Residences to deliver Leading Hotels level hospitality."

Leading Hotels of the World, representing more than 430 of the finest hotels

and resorts worldwide, is famous for its uncompromising service and quality standards. Leading Residences employs these same standards for the selection of its properties, and to determine the service levels needed at each one. Every Leading Residences home must meet an amazing 1,500 point quality checklist.

When you become a member of The Leading Residences of the World, an astonishing collection of luxury vacation homes and an equally impressive array of travel privileges are yours to command. The personalized service provided through their Leading Concierge is unparalleled in the industry.

Shannon Yachts

Introduction

Shannon Yachts are built without compromise in construction or design. They are, quite simply, the world's finest blue water sailboats.

The Company

Shannon Yachts was founded in 1975 by Walter Schulz, who dreamed of building the best blue water cruising sailboats in the world. As the sailing world knows, he succeeded at what he set out to do.

Over the years, Shannons have earned an international reputation for quality construction and offshore integrity. They have logged over a million bluewater miles, including an impressive list of circumnavigations and many transoceanic passages, mostly by husband and wife teams. Every major harbor in the world has been visited by a Shannon.

Shannon's boatbuilding experience is an unbroken, evolutionary chain from the first Shannon ever built in 1975 to the present day. During every week since the company's founding, a new Shannon has always been under construction under Schulz's personal direction. No company in the world building semi custom yachts can equal Shannon's 30 years of passagemaking records, stable management team, and consistently uncompromised standard of quality.

The craftsmen at Shannon Yachts have over three hundred combined years of experience in building quality yachts for

discriminate owners. The company's philosophy of semi custom construction allows owners to participate in the building of their dream boat from beginning of the hull layup to its commissioning by Walt Schulz in a special ceremony.

As Ferenc Máté, author of The World's Best Sailboats (Volumes I and II) put it: any boat built by Schulz is "always interesting and invariably one of the world's best yachts."

The Products

The Shannon 47 was described by Blue Water Sailing magazine as "forward thinking in concept, yet rooted in the unwavering tradition of sailing."

The Shannon 47 is the perfect boat for a couple to sail and live aboard anywhere in the world, creating an environment in which they can sail safely, comfortably, and quickly no matter how long or short the passage—and all the while maintaining a very comfortable lifestyle.

The 47 offers accommodations for up to nine. It provides excellent offshore sailing performance, balancing easily under a wide range of sea conditions and sail combinations, and it's exceptionally seaworthy. Its cockpit offers ample room, including 6' 7" long seats—giving both a place to lie down and access to a deep sail locker on the cockpit's port side. Excellent forward visibility makes this craft a pleasure to sail or dock.

A medium displacement, aft cockpit cruiser, it's available in a fixed keel or a keel centerboard hull. Its draft is reduced to 5'7" with the centerboard configuration, the choice of 90 percent

of Shannon owners (the centerboard allows for greater adjustment in the helm). The 47 has a length/displacement ratio of 227, and a sail area/displacement ratio of 17.5.

The interior arrangement and design is decided upon in consultation with the owner. But always expect the upscale, with varnished woods, quality hardware, fine leathers, and custom Kohler fixtures in the head. Storage and provisioning, considered to be of maximum importance, are built in from the start.

Macallan

Introduction

A consistent competition winner, Macallan is sometimes called "the Rolls Royce of single malts." Adhering to old style distillation methods, the Macallan is simply single malt scotch at its best.

The Company

Whisky making began as far back as the late 1700s on the land where Macallan's Easter Elchies House and distillery now stand. However, it wasn't until 1824 that the first distillation for a Macallan was recorded and licensed—probably due to the fact that, in 1823, the British Parliament eased restrictions on licensed distilleries.

The whisky region of the Spey River Valley, where Macallan resides, is known as the center of Scotland's whisky distillation. Lying between the northeastern cities of Inverness and Aberdeen, the area serves as the watershed of a huge system of rivers—the largest being the Spey, Scotland's second longest river. In the abundant countryside thereabouts, barley, the chief grain of the Macallan, is one of the principal crops.

In general, the elegant, complex Speyside single malts offer a subtle smokiness. Priding itself on adherence to traditionalist ways, Macallan has continued to use unrestructured sherry oak casks for the

aging of its single malt, resulting in a big, robust, sherryesque whisky. The Macallan is distilled on site near Easter Elchies House—the imposing building shown with pride on the label—using small, hand beaten copper stills.

The Products

The newest addition to the Macallan lineup is the Fine Oak Range—whisky matured from 8 to 30 years in American oak casks that previously contained bourbon (rather than the traditional Spanish sherry oak). This casking combination produces single malt that is delightfully smooth, delicate, and much lighter than the usual Macallan. The mesmerizing color is derived only from the interaction of spirits and wood.

The 30 year old Fine Oak is unsurpassed. Distilled in Speyside, and carefully matured for 30 long years, the pale gold whisky offers a rich and exotic nose that's reminiscent of an orange grove. On the palate: macadamia nuts, vanilla, with the slightest hints of sandalwood and black cherry.

On the youthful end of the Fine Oak scale—the youngest sibling of the 30 ,

25 , 21 , 18 , 15 , and 12 year olds—is the sprightly 10 year old. With a color like pale straw and a surprisingly complex nose, it finishes with longish hints of fruit and oak.

Many prefer a more traditional Macallan. It's less light than the Fine Oak; and, unlike most other single malts anywhere, it's aged in Spanish oak that previously held sherry. Most well known are the 12 and 18 year old expressions. More expensive, and hence less well known, are the 25 and 30 year old versions. Incidentally, the Macallan is one of the single malts used in the Famous Grouse blended whisky.

Whistler Blackcomb Ski Resort

Introduction

Heralded by avid skiers everywhere as *the* best mountains in the world, the Whistler Blackcomb ski resort has continually lived up to this high praise. The skiers' choice was validated recently when Whistler Blackcomb was chosen to host the XXI Olympic Games in 2010.

The Company

Founded by chairman and CEO Joe Houssian in 1976 as a real estate development company, Intrawest acquired Blackcomb Mountain from the Aspen Skiing Company in 1986. Ten years later, the company acquired Whistler Mountain, forming Whistler Blackcomb resort.

Today, Intrawest is the largest developer and operator of resort properties in North America and a world leader in destination resorts/adventure travel. Aside from Whistler Blackcomb, Intrawest's network includes Canadian Mountain Holidays – the world's largest heli skiing operation, Abercrombie & Kent – world leader in luxury adventure travel, Sandestin Golf and Beach Resort, Colorado's Copper Mountain and Winter Park, and Club Intrawest (a private resort club with nine North American locations).

With a network of premier properties that range from towering mountains to pristine white sand beaches, Intrawest's resorts combine the allure and beauty of nature with experiences that last a lifetime.

vacation homes, entertainment venues, restaurants, bars and shops.

Both Whistler and Blackcomb Mountains are developed for skiing, comprising the largest prime skiing terrain in all of North America (nearly 8200 acres). That's more than 50% larger than next closest Vail (about 5300 acres). The highest lift elevation is Blackcomb's (7,494 feet—1/3 of it above timberline), as is the greatest vertical drop of any resort on

Through more than 8 million annual skier visits on 10 mountains, thousands of golfers on 36 championship golf courses, and thousands more visiting lakeside and ocean beaches, Intrawest ranks among the leisure industry's leaders.

Based in Vancouver, British Columbia, Intrawest is a public company listed on the New York and Toronto stock exchanges

The Place

Whistler Blackcomb ski resort, located in Whistler, British Columbia, Canada, is composed of several "villages," each with many large hotels, condominiums,

the continent—5,280 feet. The longest run is 7 miles, the annual snowfall is 360 inches, and snowmaking equipment can cover 584 acres. Added to these amazing figures: 12 alpine bowls, three glaciers, more than 200 well marked trails, and a cutting edge lift system with 37 lifts.

The resort also offers top notch heli skiing and the world famous "Couloir Extreme" run, which, according to the gurus of Skiing Magazine, is one

of the world's top ten steep runs. But beginners needn't worry: there are plenty of beautiful, easy bunny trails.

Small wonder that Whistler Blackcomb is consistently ranked as one of world's best places to ski.

It's also a great place to après ski. The villages brim with entertainment, tasty shops, countless mouth watering restaurants, many dozens of bars and discos, and more than 100 hotels and condominiums—including the illustrious Fairmont Chateau Whistler Resort, The lavish Pan Pacific Lodge, and the new Westin Resort & Spa. Many lodgings are ski in/ski out.

La Costa Resort & Spa

Introduction

The La Costa Resort and Spa was, quite literally, America's first full service destination spa resort, opening its doors in 1965, years before "wellness" became big business. Hollywood stars and other wealthy, affluent Americans embraced the concept wholeheartedly, and a new kind of resort was born.

The resort offers more than 500 rooms, including one bedroom and two bedroom suites, four heated swimming pools, golf on two courses that have, since the 1960's, tested the greatest names in the game, an impressive athletic club, and a world class spa.

The Company

The rebirth of La Costa Resort and Spa will remind everyone of its storied reputation as the first true spa resort in the country. In 2003, this amazing property underwent an extensive multi million dollar renovation. The results include completely renovated guest rooms, a new lobby and registration area, an expansive Athletic Club featuring aerobics classes and a pilates studio, the new family pool, numerous retail shops, and the new Spa La Costa.

This brand new 42,000 square foot spa facility includes 42 treatment rooms, indoor and outdoor relaxation areas, private spa suites, and the Yamaguchi Salon. In addition, La Costa is home to the Chopra Center for Well Being, founded by renowned philosopher and health expert Deepak Chopra. It was recently voted #1 Spa in the West by *Travel & Leisure Magazine*.

This resort draws discriminating travelers from around the world. The elegant establishment displays a contemporary style architecture with red tile roofs surrounded by luscious greenery. Guest rooms are tastefully decorated with beautiful cream colored drapes, modern furniture and French doors leading to spacious balconies. Guests stay in individual rooms, suites or executive homes. The deluxe spa services include various types of body wraps, soothing skin therapies, massages and generally indulgent pampering for a fairly demanding clientele.

The golfing at La Costa is among the finest in the world, and enthralls golfers of all abilities. It has received numerous accolades from *Golf Digest, Golf Week* and *Travel & Leisure Golf* publications. When you walk the fairways, you are walking in the steps of the legends of the game. La Costa has hosted PGA Tour events over the past 40 years.

The La Costa Racquet Club offers members and guests an amazing 19 tennis courts featuring clay and hard court surfaces, with 7 courts lit for evening play. For those eager to improve their game, they have the La Costa Tennis School. Host to the annual Acura Classic on the Women's Pro Tour, this great facility is viewed by many to be one of the Top 100 Tennis Resorts in the world.

The award winning dining choices at La Costa Resort and Spa elevate California cuisine to new heights with appealingly diverse, freshly prepared culinary

offerings in picturesque settings. Three different dining options await the hungry guest – the Spa Café, Legends California Bistro and the Blue Fire Grill.

With hundreds of beautiful Spanish themed guest rooms, multiple swimming pools, a world famous spa, gourmet cuisine, and the finest in golf and tennis, this 400 plus acre property is a mecca of high times and timeless memories.

Bugatti

Introduction

Bugatti is one of the most celebrated marques of the automobile and one of the most exclusive auto producers of all time. The company is legendary for creating some of the best sports cars the world has ever seen. The original Bugatti failed with the start of World War II, but the name has been resurrected twice, and is now back on the world stage with their Bugatti Veyron.

The Company

The success of this incredible racing car goes back over eight decades. In 1924, the Bugatti Type 35 became what is probably the most successful racing car of all time with over 2,000 wins to its credit. Many victories are remembered over the years, but it was the final racing success at Le Mans that is front and center – Jean Pierre Wimille and Pierre Veyron won the 1939 race with just one car and few resources.

In 1987 an Italian entrepreneur, Romano Artioli, acquired the legendary Bugatti name and established Bugatti Automobili SpA. The new company built a factory in Campogalliano, a town near Modena, Italy. The first completed car was called the Bugatti EB110 GT, and was recognized as the most technically advanced supercar ever produced.

In 1998, Volkswagen AG purchased the rights to produce cars under the Bugatti marque. Two years later Volkswagen

founded Bugatti Automobiles SAS and introduced the Veyron concept, a 16 cylinder car that boasted over 1,000 horsepower. Development continued over the next few years into 2005, when it was announced that the Bugatti Veyron 16.4 would start delivering in early 2006.

The Products

Jeremy Clarkson of *The Sunday Times* summed up the Bugatti Veyron in only five words: "Utterly, stunningly, jaw droppingly brilliant!"

Some of the amazing facts associated with this phenomenal automobile include: at 6000 rpm the engine generates 1001 horsepower; acceleration allows it to go from zero to 60mph in less than 2.5 seconds; top speed is over 250 mph; and it sells for more than 800,000 pounds, or over $1.4 million USD. Auto experts agree on one thing – it deserves 12 stars.

The Bugatti Veyron is simply as good, and as fast, as it gets.

This car is not a half baked aftermarket or boutique road burner. It is a production car developed and tested to the standards of Volkswagen. With a top speed of 253 mph, it is also the fastest production car ever built. It covers the length of a football field in only one second!

Achieving 1,000 horsepower in a racing engine is one thing, but to do so in a reliable, durable and emissions legal configuration is truly astonishing. With about as much engine output as two Corvette Z06 V 8s, it is no surprise that the Bugatti engineers decided to go with the all wheel drive. An engine that develops four digit power throws off more heat than a dozen pizza ovens.

Consequently in the nose of the Veyron are three coolant radiators, one heat exchanger for the twin air to liquid intercoolers, and two air conditioning condensers. Unfortunately for affluent fans of the Bugatti Veyron 16.4, the company plans to build only about 50 cars per year.

Brioni Suits

Introduction

High fashion clothing company Brioni was founded in 1945 by master tailor Nazareno Fonticoli and fashion designer Gaetano Savini. They opened their first suit shop in Rome's central Via Barbaerini after the end of World War II. The company was named "Brioni" after the resort on the coast of the Adriatic Sea. From the beginning, Brioni suits were luxuries only afforded to the privileged few, namely Europe's wealthy aristocrats.

Their first fashion show, held in 1952, gained the company exposure to clients around the world.

The Company

Celebrities began to buy their suits from Brioni in the mid 1950s when Rome became a popular vacation spot for wealthy Americans. Brioni clients included Clark Gable, Gary Cooper, John Wayne, Kirk Douglas and Rock Hudson. Brioni suits have appeared in a number of James Bond movies since 1995. New York family boss John Gotti earned the name 'Dapper Don' after his extensive wardrobe of custom tailored Brioni suits. Currently, Brioni is a favorite of real estate mogul Donald Trump.

Today Brioni's 900 tailors create over 200 models in different styles and sizes each year. Fully one quarter of the production consists of made to measure tailored suits for an elite group of 25,000 clients.

The Products

Brioni was the definitive Roman tailoring establishment of the "Continental" look of the 1950s. The silhouette was immediately identifiable, with its pitched shoulders, tapered waist, and narrow hips and trousers, suggesting the architectural purity and astringency of the postwar Italian aesthetic. Brioni, with its sensitive tailoring, was one of the pioneers in the softenings of men's tailored clothing, bringing immediate pliability in slim lines and delicate drapery. The fabrics advocated by Fonticoli and Savini were borrowed from women's wear for a beautiful hand and lush suppleness which also brought color to the sober traditions of men's tailoring.

The American film stars, avatars of masculinity all, were important in introducing American men in particular to the comfort of Brioni's labor intensive and meticulous tailoring. America was very important to Brioni's image and business: the American tendency of men of big frame and naïve awkwardness was superbly civilized by the sophistication of Brioni tailoring. Moreover, America's embrace of the lean Italian style created an alliance powerful enough to serve as an alternative to Savile Row, softening the structure of the suit and allowing the heretical interventions of style and fashion to come into men's tailoring. Brioni is said to be the first men's tailor to employ raw silks and rich brocades in men's fine suits. And today, Brioni tailoring is still among the most tactile and luxurious in the world.

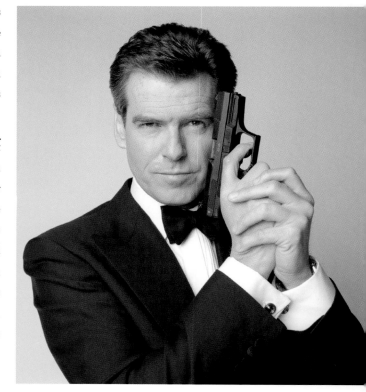

Each garment requires at least 18 hours of work, and there are more than 5,000 different fabrics to choose from. The ready to wear suits run from US$3,600 to $5,500, and the custom tailored suits from $4,000 up to $24,000. Brioni suits can be purchased at high end stores, including Saks Fifth Avenue, Bergdorf Goodman and Neiman Marcus.

Although Brioni has diversified into other categories, it continues to maintain its focus on customers it calls "luxuriants," defined as those apparel buyers who are able to interpret and appreciate luxury. The company has employed this strategy to become a $100 million international brand, with the United States representing its most important market, over 35% of total sales.

Temo Sunrooms

Introduction

TEMO Sunrooms pioneered the thermal sunroom. Early porch enclosures, popular from the 1940s through the 1970s, were made of screens attached to wood posts, or thin glass and screen walls built under aluminum awnings. These were unattractive, provided limited use, had no interior temperature control, and they did not last. In the early 1970s, TEMO introduced thermal roof and wall technology for sunrooms. This, and other innovations, solved past problems and forever evolved the definition of porch enclosures.

The Company

TEMO Sunrooms' founder and CEO, Giovanni (Nino) Vitale, immigrated to America from Italy in 1967, at the age of 22, unable to speak English. He found work fabricating aluminum skirting for manufactured homes. A born visionary, he realized homeowners loved the outdoors, but needed protection from insects and weather, with "indoor comfort" in various temperatures and seasons.

Believing that, "There is no such thing as a problem, only opportunity," Nino Vitale designed enclosures with single skin aluminum walls, built under his customers' aluminum carports. Homeowners loved them but reported condensation from the naturally occurring cold conductivity of the aluminum roofs.

This inspired the innovation of thermal sunroom roof panels – thick structural Polystyrene insulation between aluminum skins. Condensation was eliminated and Nino's sunroom manufacturing company was born, incorporating in 1971.

By 1972, TEMO engineering developed thermal window walls. High performance windows were set into insulated wall panels. The sunrooms were stronger, more comfortable and could be installed in just a day. Business boomed.

Growing, TEMO moved in 1978 to larger facilities in Clinton Township, Michigan. The manufacturing complex expanded in 1994 to include Tony V's Sunrooms & Spas, TEMO's retail showroom.

By the mid 1990s, home improvement companies in Michigan and surrounding states became the first TEMO dealers. Today, more than 150 hand selected companies sell TEMO sunrooms in the United States and Canada.

TEMO's unique sunroom business model includes factory training its dealers in design and installation for universal quality and user assurance. Dedicated in house marketing supports dealers' growth.

Vision and innovation established TEMO as the thermal sunroom leader. Homeowners now enjoy an attractive, strong, comfortable and protective outdoor space built to last.

The Product

TEMO Sunrooms' roof styles offer architectural variety to complement home styles. Choices include: studio, cathedral, split level, conservatory, solarium and an industry first sunroom hip roof. Sunrooms may be customized in size, design and glass options.

More than 50 exceptional features provide lifetime quality, maintenance free use

and excellent return on investment. For example, TEMO designed residential grade windows that withstand up to category 4 hurricanes – improving weak "storm" enclosure windows. Specialty glass controls comfort and blocks UV rays that damage interior furnishings.

TEMKOR is a nearly indestructible polymer wall surface. Sunrooms retain their "like new" appearance through decades of use and weather exposure.

Roof panels provide a total thermal barrier against the elements. An interlocking connection system and standing seam mean extraordinary performance and strength.

Sunrooms are also tested and certified, with a warranty covering the owners' lifetime – protection unique to TEMO products. Today, over 30 years later, TEMO's pioneering spirit continues, bringing ongoing evolution to the sunroom world.

© TEMO Inc. 2004

Questar Pools

Introduction

The best way to introduce this luxury product is through the eyes of the experts:

Robb Report Magazine—identified Questar Pools, and the man behind it, Skip Phillips, as internationally the single most influential pool designer.

IQ Magazine—identified Questar as the sole resource for innovative pool design on a global level.

The Franklin Report—gave Questar the best possible scores. Quality—highest imaginable; Value—worth every penny; Recommendation—my first and only choice!

The Company

Skip Phillips entered the world of pools in 1975, servicing and repairing over one thousand pools a week. Four years later, his instincts told him that he could design and build pools far superior to the ones he was maintaining. Success was instant and meteoric. The second pool he produced won a design award and since then his company, Questar Pools, has won over 100 local and international design awards, including International Best of Show.

Currently, Phillip's creations can be appreciated on the covers and pages of many magazines and books, including *Better Homes & Gardens*, *Millionaire*, *Barnes & Nobles Dream Pools*, *Custom Builder* and *Décor and Style*. Accolades abound for what many believe is the finest pool designer in the world.

class reputation on this fact and have been recognized because of it. Their commitment to innovative design, long lasting quality materials, and sound construction practices have earned them the highest honors in the industry. They firmly believe that families deserve no less than the best.

When a family decides to add a pool to their home, many good reasons contribute to their decision. Health and exercise, family leisure time, and the wonderful opportunity for entertaining are just a few. Besides providing many

Today, Skip Phillips is one of three founding partners of Genesis 3, an international design consortium that is dedicated to being the resource for those with higher expectations in waterscape design.

The Products

All Questar projects have one mark of distinction: They complement a home's architecture and conform to its natural environment. They have built a world

hours of enjoyment for the family, a pool addition also offers long term value through appreciation of their property. Maximum value is best achieved by ensuring aesthetic appeal along with the more utilitarian functions.

Today's swimming pools are much more than splashy private playgrounds; they are artful waterworks or other worldly waterscapes. Among the most popular and sophisticated pool treatments is the vanishing edge – an optical illusion also known as the disappearing edge or infinity design. Although it first appeared in France in 1870, the technical aspects of the design style have progressed light years through the fluid inspirations of Skip Phillips.

Pioneer Television

Introduction

Pioneer Corporation is a global leader in electronics and audio video products for the home, car and commerce and industry. They excel in the following core multimedia technologies – digital versatile disc (DVD), plasma display televisions and in car navigation and A/V systems.

The Company

Founded in 1938 as a manufacturer of audio products and headquartered in Toyko, Japan, Pioneer now has more than 39,000 employees worldwide. Its shares are traded on the New York Stock Exchange (ticker symbol: PIO), the Toyko Exchange, Euronext Amsterdam and the Osaka Securities Exchange.

The company's track record for developing class leading technologies has consistently attracted industry acclaim. And its continued focus on innovation remains at the heart of its drive to shape the future of its core consumer electronics markets.

Some industry firsts include: Component car stereo in 1975, GPS car navigation

with sophisticated design, Pioneer's products transport you to a world of pure enjoyment.

For two years running, Pioneer has proved itself the best of the best in Plasma Television. The Pioneer PDP 506XDE combines myriad innovations to set a new standard for plasma picture quality. Its sixth generation "Pure Black Panel" increases luminance efficiency, and decreases unwanted light output, yielding increased sharpness and contrast while reducing overall energy

in 1990, DVD/LD/CD compatible player in 1996 and their Plasma display technology in 1997.

Pioneer's ethos of "Sound. Vision. Soul" is at the heart of every aspect of its business. With the world of entertainment developing faster than ever, Pioneer's aim is to provide visionary products with the ultimate in sound and audio performance, combined with convenience and flexibility to provide the definitive entertainment experience.

The Products

Step into the world of Pioneer and experience images and sounds that you never imagined possible. By combining cutting edge technology

consumption. New Pure Drive 2HD circuitry generates deeper blacks without sacrificing detail, and a PAL specific multi step 3D Y/C filter drastically improves analogue tuner performance.

At a recent Consumer Electronics show in Las Vegas, Pioneer launched a series of audio and video products that bring new dimension to the high definition home theater experience. With one of the world's first 1080p 50inch plasma displays, one of the world's first Blu ray Disc players and best in class receivers and speakers, Pioneer unveiled technical innovation in High Definition that creates an experience never seen or heard before in a home theater.

Patron Tequila

Introduction

In 1989 two visionaries, John Paul Mitchell Systems cofounder John Paul DeJoria and entrepreneur Martin Crowley formed The Patron Spirits Company. Their singular goal was to produce "the best tequila in the world." They have succeeded beyond all expectations.

The Patron Spirits Company is dedicated to the pursuit of perfection. Since the beginning, John Paul has been collaborating with his cofounder and their staff of experts, perfecting, innovating, and setting new industry standard as his spirits continues to move towards that goal.

The Company

Son of immigrants, winner of the Horatio Alger award, philanthropist, special emissary to the United Nations Environmental Program, John Paul DeJoria is an extraordinary person and entrepreneur extraordinaire. His President and CEO is Ed Brown. The spirits business comes naturally to Ed, he was literally born into it. His father dedicated over half a century to the industry. After an early career as a golf pro on the PGA Tour, Ed decided to return to his roots. Ed brings his wealth of experience, his passion for the product and his natural competitive spirit to the company.

It all started when they took the 100% pure Waeber blue agave, grown in the hills of Jalisco Mexico, and blended traditional techniques with modern technology. The result was the world's first ultra premium tequila. Soon after, they built a new distilling factory in Jalisco. With the guidance of master distiller Francisco Alcarez, the new factory was designed to be state of the art with a core steeped in tradition.

Patron Tequila is today, the world's number one premium tequila, outselling its nearest competitor by more than 800% in the United States alone. In 2004, Patron Tequila was recognized with the American Academy of Hospitality Sciences Five Star Diamond Award. Patron is the first spirits brand ever to receive this prestigious honor. That same year it also received Impact Magazine's "Hot Brand of the Year Award."

The Products

Patron Tequila, like the great wines and cognacs of the world, is exceptional for a reason. It begins with the finest growing region in Mexico, with perfect soil and climate allowing for the sugar and acid balances to mature and produce 'Agave Pina' unequalled elsewhere in the world.

Eight distinctive products now share the Patron label: Gran Patron Platinum, Patron Anejo, Patron Reposado, Patron Silver, Patron XO Café, Patron Citronge, Pyrat Cask, and Pyrat XO Reserve. Each of them is the finest of their brand. The newest, Gran Patron Premium, is an extraordinary triple distilled pure tequila.

Once again, The Patron Spirits Company is raising the bar.

Gran Patron is considered by many to be a true connoisseur's silver tequila.

This is the smoothest sipping tequila ever produced. Called a young or "joven" tequila, Patron Silver is another ultra premium spirit. This light, fresh tequila is a favorite of connoisseurs worldwide. Patron Silver is the perfect ingredient in a margarita or mixed cocktail. Patron Reposado is aged in oak barrels for a minimum of six months. It is aged and blended to incorporate the fresh, clean taste of Patron Silver with a hint of the oak flavor found in Patron Anejo.

Hayman

Introduction

Frequently acknowledged as an Australian tourism icon and a world leader in hotel, resort and destinational excellence, the Hayman Island Resort has consistently been honoured with prestigious local and international awards. This incredible place came to our attention through a Discovery Channel program. It is today, one of the world's most acclaimed resort destinations.

The Company

The Hayman Great Barrier Reef is Australia's most celebrated private island destination, beautifully situated in the magnificent Great Barrier Reef. Hayman provides an ideal setting for both relaxing leisure activities and exciting sporting pursuits. The resort features 234 wonderfully appointed rooms, each one featuring a private terrace or balcony with magnificent views over the famous Hayman Pool, gardens, beach and lagoon.

Surrounded by idyllic coral fringed beaches and the waters of the Coral Sea, Hayman offers guests a variety of rooms, suites, penthouses and a beach villa. The accommodations, restaurants, guest service areas, marine facilities and operational plant have been designed to blend in with the natural beauty of the surroundings.

The Place

The accolades and awards that this resort has received over the last few years are far too long to list here. Some of the more noteworthy include: Conde Nast Traveler Gold List of the Best Hotels in the World six years running; Readers Travel Awards World's Top 100 also six years and counting; Forbes Magazine World's Best Beach Resort 2001; and voted #2 on Discovery Channel's Ultimate Ten Vacation Destinations.

Hayman is the first Australian resort to be inducted into the National Travel Industry Awards' Hall of Fame and Australian Tourism Awards.

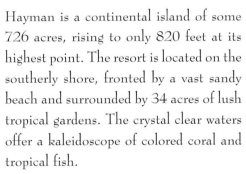

Hayman is a continental island of some 726 acres, rising to only 820 feet at its highest point. The resort is located on the southerly shore, fronted by a vast sandy beach and surrounded by 34 acres of lush tropical gardens. The crystal clear waters offer a kaleidoscope of colored coral and tropical fish.

The landscape is a beautiful blend of manicured gardens meandering throughout the resort and rugged bushland where guests can venture on an island walk to scenic lookouts and exquisite beaches.

The dining options are plentiful and the food all of gourmet quality. La Fontaine is elegant, with a formal yet relaxed atmosphere. It has a sense of grand occasion, created by a combination of soft and rich tones amid Louis XVI furnishings. Guests are treated to an exquisite selection of authentically prepared European cuisine using the best local and international produce. The wine cellars feature an impressive range of over 750 vintages from the world's premier vineyards.

Hayman remains committed to benchmark tourism excellence. In 2005, a new health experience, Spa Chakra Hayman, opened on the island offering guests an extensive selection of personally tailored beauty and well being programs utilizing the great Guerlain product range.

BELVEDERE

V O D K A

DISTILLED AND BOTTLED IN POLAND
BY POLMOS ZYRARDÓW

I M P O R T E D

40% ALC./VOL. (80 PROOF) 750ml

Belvedere Vodka

Introduction

As Poland is recognized as the birthplace of vodka, it is fitting that Belvedere is named after the Belvedere Palace, formerly home to Polish royalty and presidents. Today, Belvedere Vodka offers a luxury experience to a broad international audience of vodka enthusiasts and connoisseurs.

Belvedere Vodka hails from the small town of Zyrardow in the Mazovian plains west of Warsaw, Poland. Following traditions dating back more than 600 years, Belvedere is handcrafted in small batches to ensure superior quality meeting only the highest of standards.

The Company

First introduced to North America in 1996, Belvedere single handedly created the luxury vodka segment – now the fastest growing category in distilled spirits. Less than a decade later, Belvedere's high character and uncompromising integrity became recognized worldwide. Consumer demand continues to increase at an accelerated pace, and global recognition of the brand is at an all time high.

The Products

Belvedere's taste profile features a creamy palate, subtle sweetness and smooth, clean finish that only comes from using 100% Dakowskie Gold Rye as the single grain ingredient. It is distilled four times, the optimum number for enhancing its unique, subtle character. If a taste sampling shows even a hint of imbalance, the entire batch is discarded, and they start anew.

Nobody really knows when the flavored spirit revolution

started. Some say it began slowly in the late 1980s as a result of the melding of global tastes and cultures. Others say it gained momentum in the 1990s when a new generation of inspired young chefs demanded the freshest local ingredients for their creations. What is certain is the huge appetite for flavors has become a way of life.

Belvedere's quest to redefine the flavor category started in 1999. Their goal to create a luxury vodka infused with real fruit flavor led them to renowned European flavor artist, Elie Arnaud Denoix, who shared their passion for creating natural fruit flavors. The House of Denoix is one of the leading producers to offer high quality flavors. The rustic 16th century village of Collonges la Rouge is located in southern France. Elie Arnaud looks for four things in fruits he uses to flavor vodka: soil, sun, variety and the love of the grower.

Macerating, or steeping, is the flavoring process used for capturing the purest natural flavor from fruit. Real fruit is combined with Belvedere Vodka for weeks, during which time Elie is constantly tasting and adjusting for the ideal balance of flavors. He calls this shading, and it is similar to an artist using a palette to create color. Belvedere's new Cytrus and Pomarancza flavors are classic examples of this art.

Handcrafted using lemons grown in the sunny citrus groves near Murcia, Spain, and limes harvested nearby in southeastern Spain, Belvedere Cytrus expresses the lively character of natural lemon with exotic layers of lime.

Distilled using ripe Spanish mandarins, Moroccan oranges and exotic Moroccan orange blossoms with limes also from Spain, Belvedere Pomarancza shows deep orange aromas with bursts of orange blossom. Notes of sweet oranges are balanced by an elegant touch of lime.

Rolex

Introduction

Founded in 1905 by Hans Wilsdorf, Rolex is a brand of Swiss watch renowned for its superior quality and exclusivity, as well as its cost. Their timepieces range in price from around $5,000 to more than $100,000. The watches have become status symbols of the rich and famous – as well as the upwardly mobile career minded individual. Although a symbol of success,)) has earned its strong reputation through innovations in design and function over the past century.

The Company

Over the years, Rolex has enjoyed a succession of achievements in watchmaking technology: the world's first Certificate of Accuracy awarded to a wristwatch; the world's first truly waterproof watch case called the Oyster; the invention of the automatic winding mechanism with "Perpetual" rotor. The list of achievements is long, with the greatest of these being Rolex's commitment to the pioneering spirit of its founder and continuing to improve upon the exceptional quality of its watches.

Among the more prominent of the company's innovations are the first self winding watch; the first waterproof watch; the first wristwatch with a date on the dial; the first watch to show two time zones at once; and most importantly the first watchmakers to earn the coveted chronometer certification for a wristwatch. To date, Rolex still holds the record for the most certified chronometer movements in the category of wristwatches.

primary bracelets for the Rolex Oyster line are named Jubilee, Oyster and the President. Rolex "dressy" watches are from their Cellini line.

As everyone knows, Rolex watches are often counterfeited and sold in markets around the world that cater to tourists. These fakes are mainly produced in

The Products

Rolex has three distinct watch lines in Rolex, Tudor and Cellini. Among the modern Rolex Oyster watch models are the Air King, Datejust, GMT Master II, Explorer, Submariner, Sea Dweller, Yacht Master and the Oyster Perpetual. The

China, and retail from $5 upward. One good test to determine if the Rolex is a fraud can be performed simply by looking at it. Most Rolex models have a self winding mechanism movement, which allows the second hand to move smoothly around the watch face, while the cheaply made fakes are a simple battery powered quartz movement which "ticks" from one second indicator to the next. The old adage "you get what you pay for" certainly rings true here.

Rolex has a philanthropic tradition of supporting exceptional talent, quality and achievement. The Rolex Institute aims at sharing the recognition of individuals who, through their initiatives, excel in their chosen fields, making a meaningful contribution to the world in which we live. The Rolex Awards were established in 1976 to encourage a spirit of enterprise in individuals from around the world. Unlike other programs that recognize past achievements, the Rolex Awards assist men and women in implementing ongoing projects. The Awards fund projects in the realms of science, technology, exploration, the environment and cultural heritage.

Sonora Resort

Introduction

The sparkling waters dotted with picturesque isles on the west coast of British Columbia are world famous. The definitive place to center yourself here has emerged as the ultimate wilderness retreat – Sonora Resort. They offer five star accommodations, an extraordinary level of attention, and a breathtaking outdoor adventure without compromise.

The Company

Sonora represents a new level of resort that does not limit itself to one pursuit but opens up the range of unforgettable possibilities – sport and fly fishing, kayaking, extraordinary spa and wellness treatments, and wilderness outings including eye opening tours overlooking the Grizzly Bear Habitat.

For discerning travelers who desire the wilderness experience in an exquisite luxury setting there are simply no equivalents to Sonora Resort. Less than an hour by helicopter or seaplane from Vancouver, British Columbia, this unique place is a wholly original West Coast jewel.

The Place

Inspired by one of the most pristine natural environments on earth (and water) the core idea of Sonora is to provide experiences, both indoor and outdoor, that live up to the spectacular vistas.

That attitude has resulted in a passionate pursuit of service excellence that is ultra professional and warmly personal at the same time. When you arrive on the dock by boat, float plane or on the nearby helicopter pad, the feeling that you are part of something extremely special is overwhelming.

Dining here on gourmet Pacific Northwest cuisines from either the resident decorated chef Mathew Stowe or one of his famed contemporaries—like visiting chef Rob Feenie, winner of Iron Chef America 2005—will create memories that last a lifetime.

Some people are introduced to Sonora through small business gatherings or special events with family and friends. The facilities include a native longhouse, a new conference center, a conservatory, and individual lodges.

Others come as couples looking to connect to nature (and each other) in settings like hot tubs on open decks with the ocean just below, trails with eagles perching on trees (some of these are long term Sonora residents), and in luxury lodges that combine elegance with sumptuous country comforts and unparalleled panoramas.

There are no typical days but one can easily imagine going fishing with a trusted guide on a new Grady White—one of many in the Sonora fleet, or getting a massage—one of the treatments that make the spa at Sonora a destination in itself.

Eco tours have become extremely popular, as the fascination of seeing British Columbia wildlife up close and personal is undeniable. Casual observation of sea lions, eagles, hawks, otters, that begins

with a pair of the Sonora's binoculars, soon turns guests into avid photographers and naturalists.

A day trip to nearby Storey Creek, winner of the Golf Digest "Places to Play" designation is part of many guests' itineraries. More intriguing to many are heli hiking and heli picnic outings to coastal settings simply not accessible by any other means.

Other enjoyments at Sonora Resort include inviting private lounges, the pleasures of practicing your swing on the range golf simulator, and seafood tapas overlooking the bay.

Chateau Lafite Rothschild

Introduction

Chateau Lafite Rothschild is a winery in France currently owned by members of the Rothschild banking family. The name "Lafite" comes from the Gascon term 'la hite' meaning small hill. Only four wine producing Chateaux of Bordeaux achieved the much coveted First Growth status in the famous 1855 Classification. Of those, the first one and perhaps the most famous is Chateau Lafite Rothschild, a consistent producer of one of the world's greatest and most expensive red wines.

The Company

Situated in the great wine producing village of Pauillac in the Medoc region to the northwest of Bordeaux, the estate has been occupied since at least the 14th century. In the 17th century, the property of Chateau Lafite was purchased by the Segur family, including the 16th century manor house that still stands today. Although vines almost certainly existed on the site, around 1680 Jacques de Segur planted the majority of the famous vineyard.

In the early 18th century, Marquis Nicolas Alexandre de Segur refined the wine making techniques of the estate, and introduced his wines to the upper echelons of European society. Before long he was known as the "Wine Prince", and the wine of Chateau Lafite called "The King's Wine" thanks to the influential support of the Marechal de Richelieu. Towards the end of the 18th century, Lafite's reputation among the world's finest wines was assured and even Thomas Jefferson, when visiting Bordeaux, became a lifelong fan.

this, the bottles have no labels, for the moisture would make them disintegrate. Individual bins and sections of the cellar are identified by vintage dates, and not until the bottles are ready for shipping do they receive their labels.

Special guests are invited to see a small section known as "the library", in which vintages from as early as 1797 are kept. These old bottles are moved only to be recorked every 25 years and, because of

The Products

The wine of Chateau Lafite is a blend of four different types of grapes – Cabernet Sauvignon, Cabernet Franc, Merlot and Petite Verdot, making the wine soft and delicate in character. And, because Lafite uses generous amounts of Merlot it tends to mature a bit earlier than wines dominated by Cabernet Sauvignon. Despite this softness, the wine does not reach its peak for at least a decade after the harvest.

The cellars of this great chateau are cool and so damp that water constantly oozes from the walls and ceilings. Because of

the cool and consistent temperature, the wines remain in very good condition. Occasionally one of these old Lafites turn up at auction and fetch upwards of 100,000 pounds sterling. But due to the rapid temperature changes and movement during transport, they are of doubtful quality for drinking. Most are generally set aside for show.

The wines of Chateau Lafite are big but not overwhelming, delicate but not light and have an extraordinary balance and elegance. Most connoisseurs agree that the wine has a bouquet that is rich in almonds and violets, a richness that is incomparable and a body that clearly shows its high breeding. When describing the best vintage wines of Chateau Lafite, it is very difficult not to use superlatives. One critic wrote that the character of the wine can best be described as "the perfection of elegance".

Rosehill Wine Cellars

Introduction

Wine is enjoyed by millions around the world because of its underlying complexity. The complexity comes from the many variables in the process. It is a process that starts with the vines, the soil and the climate, and ends with storage. All stages are equally important to a fine wine experience.

The Company

Rosehill Wine Cellars are designers and builders of custom wine cellars. They are also a key distributor of wine racking systems and wine cooling units. Rosehill was initially established as a general renovation company in 1983. In 1995, they built their first wine cellar, and Gary LaRose immediately realized that this was the field he had a passion for.

So he decided to specialize in it. Since that time, they have expanded to include a vast array of wine storage products.

The single goal of Rosehill Wine Cellars is to be one of the top companies in North America supplying beautiful high quality products for wine storage. They are now considered by many to be a top tier builder of custom wine cellars. Their competitive edge is product knowledge.

They make several different Wine Cabinets: LeCache – their premier unit made with cherry wood or maple, storing from 172 to 622 bottles; La Sommeliere – a European style wine cabinet featuring quiet operation, that can be built in kitchens; Cavavin – offers deluxe and built in cabinets in solid wood or stainless steel with many great options; Small Wine Cabinets – countertop

This becomes quickly obvious when you come across their concise and informative Wine Care Guide on their website.

The Products

Rosehill offers wine coolers, wine cabinets and wine refrigerators for all needs and applications. Their wide selection of wine coolers offers the finest in cabinet and refrigerator performance. These attractive and durable products are crafted to provide customers with the perfect glass of wine, for any and every occasion.

and built in models that will hold 6 to 45 bottles.

They also craft a fine line of Wine Racks: Modular Redwood – is their most popular line of wine rack, these all heart redwood beauties are easy to install; 7 ft Premium Kit—using premium redwood, western red cedar, or Malaysian mahogany—these wine racks are extremely high quality.

These units are deeper, so the necks of bottles are completely submerged. They pride themselves on offering the ultimate in Custom Made Wine Racks. Rosehill will work with your room dimensions to create a true custom fit from wall to wall and floor to ceiling. The end result is a showcase wine cellar for your prize collection of wines.

Lurssen

Introduction

The Lurssen shipyard is a family business now in its fourth generation. Now well into their second century, Lurssen has earned a reputation worldwide for its high class custom built super yachts. The combination of constant innovation, the high quality of work, the dedicated workforce, its discretion, and the close interaction with the clients have kept them dominant in the world of the luxury yacht.

The Company

In 1875, upon opening for business, Friedrich Lurssen stated: "My firm shall be known as a leader in both quality and performance." It has remained their policy throughout their long and proud history. After all, the family name is on every ship.

The company grew large with small boats – developing from a modest boatbuilding shed to a world leader in yachts, naval ships and other special purpose vessels. Small work boats were their specialty for the first 15 years. In 1890, the firm successfully built and sold rowing boats for sports clubs, then became a pioneer for motorboats in Germany. In 1912, a Lurssen speedboat, with Otto Lurssen at the helm, won a number of prizes in the prestigious Monaco Race.

The shipyard is divided into three separate fields. The first is the building of naval vessels and special watercraft, like

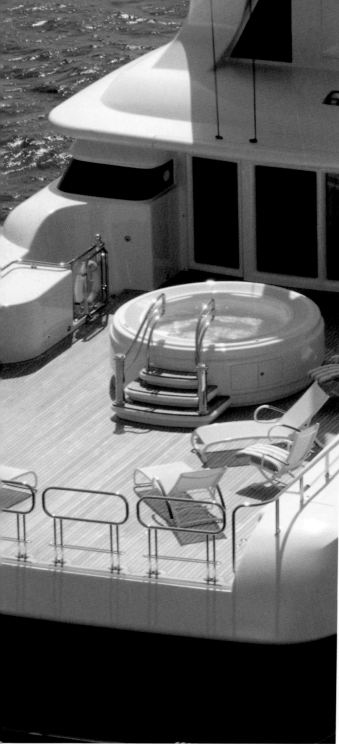

fast patrol boats, corvettes and support vessels. The second area is the building of luxury super yachts. These range from 40 meters to more than 150 meters in size. The third field is the Lurssen Logistic. It concentrates on all logistical parts of the group – repair and maintenance, yacht management, parts documentation, crew training center and the training simulator.

To realize the special demands of their clients, Lurssen works with cutting edge designers from all over the world. They interact with the shipyard staff of more than 100 naval architects and engineers in order to seek creative options and design solutions to attain the highest quality and technical standards.

The Products

With more than 3,000 ships and 130 years behind them, Lurssen's excellence in ship design is unparalleled. A custom computer design program for a three dimensional CAD System is accessed by a staff of naval architects and engineers.

From this, workshop drawings for hulls, decks and interiors can be implemented with the utmost precision. The Lurssen design group is also called upon for cooperative ventures. The staff will collaborate with owners and outside designers in finding creative options and solutions to exterior and interior plans. Practical seagoing essentials are married with technological advances and aesthetic elements of grace and beauty.

While much high technology can be applied to the design, engineering and speed factors of a yacht, Lurssen remains respectful of the traditional values which must be applied to interior work requiring master craftsmen. In seeking the perfect translation of specifications of their yacht interiors, Lurssen works with many interior designers. Teams of craftsmen, many of whom have followed their fathers and grandfathers into the trade, handcraft the moldings, polish the wood to perfection, and lay the marble in ways that can never be replaced by modern machinery.

Corporate Information

Alienware Corporation
Miami, Florida
www.alienware.com

BeefEater BBQs
New South Wales, Australia
www.beefeaterbbq.com

Bellagio
Las Vegas, Nevada
www.bellagio.com

Belvedere Vodka
Zyrardow, Poland
www.belvederevodka.com

Bertram Yacht
Miami, Florida
www.bertram.com

Brioni
Rome, Italy
www.brioni.it

Broyhill Furniture
Lenoir, North Carolina
www.broyhillfurn.com

Brunswick Billiards
Bristol, Wisconsin
www.brunswickbilliards.com

Bugatti
Molsheim, France
www.bugatti cars.de

Champagne Roederer
Reims, France
www.champagne-roederer.com

Chanel
Neuilly-sur-Seine, France
www.chanel.com

Chateau Lafite Rothschild
Paris, France
www.lafite.com

Chateau les Crayeres
Reims, France
www.lescrayeres.com

Crystal Cruises
Los Angeles, California
www.crystalcruises.com

De Beers
Johannesburg, South Africa
www.debeers.com

Featherlite Luxury Coaches
Sanford, Florida
www.featherlitecoaches.com

Gulfstream Jets
Savannah, Georgia
www.gulfstream.com

Harley-Davidson
Milwaukee, Wisconsin
www.harleyd-avidson.com

Hatteras Yachts
New Bern, North Carolina
www.hatterasyachts.com

Hayman Island Resort
New South Wales, Australia
www.hayman.com.au

Hennessy Cognac
Cognac, France
www.hennessy-cognac.com

The Homestead
Hot Springs, Virginia
www.thehomestead.com

John Paul Mitchell Systems
Santa Clarita, California
www.paulmitchell.com

La Costa Resort and Spa
La Quinta, California
www.lacosta.com

La Maison du Chocolat
Nanterre, France
www.lamaisonduchocolat.com

Lalique
Paris, France
www.cristallalique.fr

Le Creuset
Fresnoy-le-Grand, France
www.lecreuset.com

Louis Vuitton
Paris, France
www.louisvuitton.com

LRW Club
Dallas, Texas
www.lrwclub.com

Lurssen Yachts
Bremen Vegesack, Germany
www.lurssen.com

Macallan Scotch
Craigellachie, Scotland
www.themacallan.com

Maserati
Modena, Italy
www.maserati.com

Montblanc
Hamburg, Germany
www.montblanc.com

Napoleon Fireplaces
Ontario, Canada
www.napoleonfireplaces.com

Patron Spirits Company
Las Vegas, Nevada
www.patronspirits.com

Pebble Beach Resorts
Pebble Beach, California
www.pebblebeach.com

Pioneer Corporation
Tokyo, Japan
www.pioneer.co.uk

Questar Pools
Escondido, California
www.questarpools.com

Roche-Bobois
Paris, France
www.roche-bobois.com

Rolex
Geneva, Switzerland
www.rolex.com

Rosehill Wine Cellars
Toronto, Canada
www.rosehillwinecellars.com

St. Croix Rods
Park Falls, Wisconsin
www.stcroixrods.com

Shannon Yachts
Bristol, Rhode Island
www.shannonyachts.com

Sonora Resort
Vancouver, Canada
www.sonoraresort.com

Sound Solutions
Culver City, California
www.soundsolutions.com

Stone Brewing Company
Escondido, California
www.stonebrew.com

Temo Sunrooms
Clinton Township, Michigan
www.temosunrooms.com

Tempur Pedic
Lexington, Kentucky
www.tempurpedic.com

Thos. Baker
Bainbridge Island, Washington
www.thosbaker.com

Tiffany & Co.
New York, New York
www.tiffany.com

Treetops Lodge & Estate
Rotorua, New Zealand
www.treetops.co.nz

Versace
Milan, Italy
www.versace.com

Wedgwood
Staffordshire, U.K.
www.wedgwood.com

West Coast Fishing Club
Queen Charlotte Islands, Canada
www.westcoastfishingclub.com

Whistler Blackcomb
Whistler, Canada
www.whistlerblackcomb.com